KU-235-457

A Modernist Reader

MODERNISM IN ENGLAND 1910–1930

EDITED BY

Peter Faulkner

B. T. BATSFORD LTD · LONDON

820.900912   FAU

LIVERPOOL POLYTECHNI
C.F. MOTT CAMPUS
LIBRARY

211094/88

Selection and editorial matter
© Peter Faulkner 1986

First published 1986

All rights reserved. No part of this publication
may be reproduced, in any form or by any means,
without permission from the Publisher.

Typeset by Progress Filmsetting
London EC2
and printed in Great Britain by
Billings Ltd., Worcester

Published by B. T. Batsford Ltd
4 Fitzhardinge Street, London W1H 0AH

British Library Cataloguing in Publication Data

A Modernist reader: modernism in England 1910-1930.
1. Modernism (Literature) 2. English literature—20th century—History
and criticism
I. Faulkner, Peter
820.9'00912   PR478.M6

ISBN 0-7134-5174-2
ISBN 0-7134-5175-0 Pbk

Contents

Acknowledgements

I am grateful to the following publishers for permission to make use of copyright material:

Michael B. Yeats, Macmillan London Ltd. and Macmillan, Inc. for extracts from W.B. Yeats's 'Letter to Lady Gregory', from *Yeats. Selected Criticism* edited by N. Jeffares;

The Carcanet Press and the estate of Edgell Rickword for C.H. Rickword's 'A Note on Fiction' from Edgell Rickword's *Essays and Opinions 1921-31*, edited by Alan Young;

Routledge and Kegan Paul and Harcourt Brace Jovanovich, Inc. for I.A. Richards's 'The Poetry of T.S. Eliot' from *The Principles of Literary Criticism;*

Constable Publishers for the Preface to *Some Imagist Poets* (1915);

Chatto and Windus/The Hogarth Press and Harcourt Brace Jovanovich, Inc. for Virginia Woolf's 'Modern Fiction' and 'Mr. Bennett and Mrs Brown';

Faber and Faber and Harcourt Brace Jovanovich, Inc. for T.S. Eliot's 'Tradition and the Individual Talent', 'The Metaphysical Poets' and '*Ulysses*' Order and Myth, from *The Selected Prose of T.S. Eliot;*

Jonathan Cape, The Viking Press and the Executors of the James Joyce Estate for an extract from *A Portrait of the Artist as a Young Man;*

Harper and Row, Publishers, Inc. for an extract by Wyndham Lewis from BLAST;

Faber and Faber and New Directions Publishing Corporation for Ezra Pound's 'A Retrospect' and 'Wyndham Lewis' from *The Literary Essays of Ezra Pound*. Copyright 1935 by Ezra Pound.

A Chronology

of Publications 1910-1930

CRITICAL	CREATIVE
1910	
Pound, *The Spirit of Romance*	Forster, *Howards End*
	Yeats, *The Green Helmet and Other Poems*
1911	
Wells, 'The Contemporary Novel'	Conrad, *Under Western Eyes*
	Lawrence, *The White Peacock*
	Pound, *Canzoni*
1912	
Hueffer (Ford), *The Critical Attitude*	Lawrence, *The Trespasser*
Flint, 'Contemporary French Poetry'	Pound, *Ripostes*
Yeats, *The Cutting of an Agate*	
1913	
Flint, 'Imagisme' (Chicago)	Lawrence, *Love Poems, and Others*
Hueffer (Ford), *Henry James*	Lawrence, *Sons and Lovers*
Pound, 'A Few Don'ts...'	
1914	
Bell, *Art*	Conrad, *Chance*
James, 'The Younger Generation'	Joyce, *Dubliners*
James, *Notes on Novelists*	Yeats, *Responsibilities*
1915	
Lowell(?), Preface to *Some Imagist Poets 1915*	Aldington and H.D., *Images, Old and New*

CRITICAL	CREATIVE
	Conrad, *Victory*
	Flint, *Cadences*
	Ford, *The Good Soldier*
	Lawrence, *The Rainbow*
	Dorothy Richardson, *Pointed Roofs*
	Woolf, *The Voyage Out*
1916	
Lowell(?), Preface to *Some Imagist Poets 1916*	Joyce, *A Portrait of the Artist as a Young Man*
Middleton Murry, *Fyodor Dostoievsky: a Critical Study*	Lawrence, *Amores*
	Pound, *Cathay*
	Pound, *Lustra*
1917	
	Eliot, *Prufrock and Other Observations*
	Lawrence, *Look! We Have Come Through*
	Pound, *Homage to Sextus Propertius*
	Yeats, *The Wild Swans at Coole*
1918	
Pound, *Pavannes and Divisions*	Joyce, *Exiles*
	Lawrence, *New Poems*
	Lewis, *Tarr*
	Strachey, *Eminent Victorians*
1919	
Eliot, 'Tradition and the Individual Talent'	Eliot, *Poems*
Woolf, 'Modern Fiction'	Woolf, *Night and Day*
Yeats, 'A Letter to Lady Gregory'	
1920	
Eliot, *The Sacred Wood: Essays on Poetry and Criticism*	Pound, *Hugh Selwyn Mauberley*
Fry, *Vision and Design*	Lawrence, *The Lost Girl*
Lawrence, Introduction to *New Poems* (New York)	Lawrence, *Women in Love* (New York)
Murry, *Aspects of Literature*	
Pound, *Instigations*	

CRITICAL	CREATIVE

1921

Eliot, 'The Metaphysical Poets'
Lubbock, *The Craft of Fiction*
Murry, *The Problem of Style*

Yeats, *Michael Robartes and the Dancer*
Yeats, *Four Plays for Dancers*

1922

Murry, *Countries of the Mind*
Ogden and Richards, *The Foundations of Aesthetics*

Eliot, *The Waste Land*
Joyce, *Ulysses* (Paris)
Lawrence, *Aaron's Rod*
Woolf, *Jacob's Room*

1923

Eliot, '*Ulysses*, Order and Myth'
Lawrence, *Studies in Classic American Literature*
Lawrence, 'Surgery for the Novel –or a Bomb?'
Ogden and Richards, *The Meaning of Meaning*
Yeats, *Plays and Controversies*

Lawrence, *Birds, Beasts and Flowers*
Lawrence, *Kangaroo*

1924

Aldington, *Literary Studies and Reviews*
Eliot, *Homage to John Dryden*
Hulme, *Speculations,* ed. H. Read
Richards, *Principles of Literary Criticism*
Woolf, 'Mr. Bennett and Mrs. Brown'
Yeats, *Essays*

Ford, *Some Do Not*
Forster, *A Passage to India*

1925

Lawrence, 'Morality and the Novel'
Lawrence, 'Why the Novel Matters'
Woolf, *The Common Reader*
Yeats, *A Vision*

Eliot, *Poems 1909-25*
Ford, *No More Parades*
Woolf, *Mrs. Dalloway*

1926

Muir, *Transition: Essays in Contemporary Literature*
Read, *Reason and Romanticism*
C.H. Rickword, 'A Note on Fiction'

Ford, *A Man Could Stand Up*
Lawrence, *The Plumed Serpent*

11

CRITICAL

Richards *Principles of Literary
    Criticism*, 2nd Edn. with
    Appendices, inc.
    'The Poetry of T.S. Eliot'

CREATIVE

1927

Forster, *Aspects of the Novel*
Graves and Riding, *A Survey of
    Modernist Poetry*
Woolf, 'The Narrow Bridge of Art'

Woolf, *To the Lighthouse*

1928

Eliot, *The Sacred Wood*, 2nd Edn.
Muir, *The Structure of the Novel*
Read, *English Prose Style*
Read, *Phases of English Poetry*
E. Rickword, ed., *Scrutinies:
    Critical Essays*

Ford, *Last Post*
Lawrence, *Lady Chatterley's Lover*
Lewis, *The Childermass*
Woolf, *Orlando*
Yeats, *The Tower*

1929

Ford, *The English Novel* (New York)
Lawrence, 'Pornography and
    Obscenity'
Read, *The Sense of Glory: Essays in
    Criticism*
Richards, *Practical Criticism*
Woolf, *A Room of One's Own*

Lawrence, *Pansies*
Yeats, *The Winding Stair*

1930

Lawrence, 'A propos of
    Lady Chatterley's Lover'

Eliot, *Ash Wednesday*
Lewis, *The Apes of God*

Introduction

Looking back from the late twentieth century, we can see the arts of the period 1910-1930 as having a clear cultural identity to which the term 'Modernist' can reasonably be applied, although it was not a term used at the time. The characteristics of this movement, which affected all the arts and many countries, have been the subject of much discussion, but perhaps the neatest formulation remains that of Stephen Spender in *The Struggle of the Modern* in 1963, where he writes of modern art as 'that in which the artist reflects awareness of an unprecedented modern situation in its form and idiom.'[1] The challenge was to create new types of art which could express the bewildering but exciting complexity of the rapidly changing world. And these new forms were triumphantly created in all the arts: by Picasso, by Stravinsky, by Proust and, in the literary culture on which this anthology is focused, by Pound, Eliot, Lawrence, Woolf, Joyce and Yeats. The masterpieces of that period rightly continue to attract our attention: we cannot find in other writers of the time anything to match the achievements of the Modernists: 'Homage to Sextus Propertius' (1917), 'Hugh Selwyn Mauberley' (1920); *Prufrock, and Other Observations (1917)*, *Poems* (1919), *The Waste Land* (1922); *The Rainbow* (1915), *Women in Love* (1920); *A Portrait of the Artist as a Young Man* (1916), *Ulysses* (1922); *Jacob's Room* (1922), *Mrs. Dalloway* (1925), *To the Lighthouse* (1927); 'The Tower' (1928). This creative achievement was accompanied by a great surge of critical activity. New methods were actively propounded and defended in numerous small literary magazines, and the old methods as directly challenged and attacked. The purpose of this anthology is to make available the most significant contributions to the Modernist side of the debate, so that students of the period may be in a position to relate practice to theory. The main articles are presented complete, and no attempt has been made to minimise the disagreements between the writers concerned–Lawrence, in particular, can be seen as defining a characteristically independent position. Nevertheless there is a coherence of concern which makes these arguments mutually illuminating, especially in the context of their less-known but important contemporaries.

There is a considerable difference between the critical writings of the two decades contained in this anthology, which has been well described by Malcolm Bradbury. As he put it when writing of *The Calendar of Modern Letters*, an important magazine of the 1920s:

> On the whole, the significant activity of the little magazines of the previous decade had been that of accomplishing a literary revolution. The tone of the important journals was *avant-garde*: their circulation was small; they were addressed largely to a bohemian-intellectual reading public. Such criticism as appeared in these magazines tended to be written by literary practitioners, like Pound and Eliot, Ford Madox Hueffer and F.S. Flint, and was very much devoted to what Pound called Making It New. It was reformatory rather than considered; but it offered many critical insights that subsequent critics sought to pursue with greater precision. The twenties were a period of *critical* revolution.[2]

The contrast may not have been quite so neat (as we shall see in discussing the publication of the later criticism), but it is basically valid. The first decade is dominated by writers keen to articulate and justify their new procedures, of whom Ezra Pound is the most dramatic example. The relevant magazines are *The New Age* (edited by A.R. Orage); *The English Review* (Ford Madox Hueffer; he changed his name to Ford in 1919, and will subsequently be referred to as F.M. Ford); *Rhythm*, and later *The Blue Review* (both edited by John Middleton Murry); BLAST (edited by Wyndham Lewis); *The Egoist* (edited by Richard Aldington); and *Poetry Review*–later *Poetry and Drama* (edited by Harold Munro). At this stage the characteristic work is the article or essay rather than the book–though many of the 'books' of the 1920s were in fact collections of essays.

The texts chosen for inclusion here represent the four writers referred to by Bradbury–Ford and Flint, Pound and Eliot–together with Henry James, an established writer who may be seen as a precursor of Modernism, Wyndham Lewis (painter and writer) and T.E. Hulme (poet and critic). There is also an extract (No. 9) from James Joyce's *A Portrait of the Artist as a Young Man* (1916). Joyce differs from the other Modernists in having produced little literary criticism after his student days. What he did do, however, was to introduce discussions of criticism and aesthetics into his fictional works, usually through the semi-autobiographical figure of Stephen Dedalus. Stephen first appeared in a draft written around 1904-6, the first part of which Joyce destroyed but the remainder of which was published by Theodore Spencer in 1944 as *Stephen Hero*. In this draft Stephen is an aspiring writer. He gives a lecture on aesthetics to his college literary society, having discussed it previously with the President of the University. At the end of their conversation, the President remarks: 'Begin to look at the bright side of things, Mr. Dedalus. Art should be healthy first of all.'[3] This over-simplification is typical of the lack of understanding with which his views are received. Later Stephen observes a trivial incident in the street, and its triviality 'made him think of collecting many such moments together in a book of epiphanies. By an epiphany he meant a sudden spiritual manifestation, whether in vulgarity of speech or of gesture or in a memorable phase of the mind itself.'[4] Stephen explains his idea of the epiphany to his student friend Cranly, going on to develop his aesthetic theory from the ideas of Thomas Aquinas, the Catholic philosopher, but feels that he has aroused Cranly's hostility. Joyce rewrote these scenes for *A Portrait*, now omitting the idea of the ephiphany but keeping the context of the sceptical friend. His later formulation emphasises the ideal of the impersonality of the writer, which is central to the Modernist aesthetic. It had been well summarized by Henry James in a review of Flaubert's correspondence in 1893, in which Flaubert's own words are translated:

> His constant refrain in his letters is the impersonality, as he calls it, of the artist, whose work should consist exclusively of his subject and his style, without an emotion, an idiosyncracy that is not transformed ... 'The artist must be present in his work like God in Creation, invisible and almighty, everywhere felt but nowhere seen.'[5]

As far as fiction is concerned, Modernism may be seen to have developed from the highly conscious activity, the devotion to an ideal of Art, which Henry James (with complex reservations) took over from the great French novelist. Unlike Joyce, James was a very active critic throughout his long career as a novelist. In numerous articles and reviews he asserted the view that the novelist should be a conscious artist, developing this idea also in the series of 18 Prefaces which he wrote for the New York edition of his *Novels and Tales* (1907-9). James was no narrow formalist, but he did believe that Flaubert's *Madame Bovary* was 'a classic because the thing, such as it is, is ideally *done*, and because it shows that in such doing eternal beauty may dwell.'[6] James made his view particularly clear in two letters to Hugh Walpole, a younger novelist, in which the gracious tone of the personal sections contrasts strongly with the firmness of the critical attitude asserted (Nos. 1 and 2). James is the proponent of composition and form, of the novel as a deliberate work of art. In addition, James's stress on projecting a novel through the consciousness of one of the characters rather than through an omniscient narrator was to prove attractive to the next generation. In the Preface to *The Portrait of a Lady* James gave a retrospective account of his method in that novel: '"Place the centre of the subject in the young woman's own consciousness", I said to myself, "and you get as interesting and beautiful a difficulty as you could wish."'[7] Not all later novelists might share James's enthusiasm for 'difficulty', for the challenge of a demanding subject to the writer's power of formal control, but many were to follow his emphasis on consciousness.

Ford Madox Ford had founded *The English Review* in 1909 to give expression to writers with new approaches. He strongly criticised Edwardian culture for its materialistic commercialism and argued for cultural change. In *The Critical Attitude* (No. 4)–which he published in 1911 from a series in *The English Review*–he divided the leading contemporary writers into two groups, 'the great mainstream of European International Literature', represented by James and Conrad, and 'the temperamentally British novel' of Wells and Kipling. But his conclusion was the very liberal one that the novelist should 'strive to fulfil what he may regard as the particular canon of his Art.'[8] Later writers like Woolf were to employ the idea of contrasting traditions of novelists in a more polemical way.

Since this anthology is devoted to criticism by the Modernists, it is worth noting that H.G. Wells, presented by them as a kind of traditionalist, actually saw himself as an innovator. He was well aware of the difference between his view of fiction and that of James, and expressed it in a lecture to the Times Book Club in 1911 on 'The Scope of the Novel'. He published a revised version of the lecture as 'The Contemporary Novel' in *The Fortnightly Review* in November 1911. Wells's argument is that since the time of Dickens the novel had been going through a phase of 'narrowing and restriction', but was now recovering its spaciousness, returning to 'the lax freedom of form, the rambling discursiveness, the right to roam, of the earlier English novel, of *Tristram Shandy* and of *Tom Jones*.'[9] Wells sees the novel not so much as an art but as 'the only medium through which we can discuss the great majority of the problems which are being raised in such bristling multitude by our contemporary social developments.'[10] Wells is making high claims for the novel, but in terms of its social utility:

> You can see now the scope of the claim I am making for the novel; it is to be the social mediator, the vehicle of understanding, the instrument of

self-examination, the parade of morals, and the exchange of manners, the factory of customs, the criticism of laws and institutions and of social dogmas and ideas. It is to be the home confessional, the initiator of knowledge, the seed of fruitful self-questioning.[11]

Wells concluded that this kind of writing with its direct social commitment would 'appeal to the young and the hopeful and the curious, against the established, the dignified, the defensive.'[12] It is ironical that Wells himself was to seem representative of established attitudes to the younger novelists, who were closer to James in insistence on the art of the novel rather than on its value in promoting discussion of social issues.

James, about whom Ford published a largely admiring book in 1913, presented his side of the argument strongly, if with characteristic urbanity, in two review articles in *The Times Literary Supplement* in March and April 1914 (No. 3). Here he praises Wells and Arnold Bennett for their solid depiction of their worlds, but raises the question of where the central interest of their work is to be located amid the wealth of local material. The novelist, it is implied, must not simply present the reader with a mass of accurately rendered material; he must also organise that material in an illuminating way. It is to further elucidation of the principles of that organisation that the Modernist novelists, particularly Joyce and Woolf, were to devote themselves. Traditional English reliance on the author's personal feelings or experiences no longer seemed adequate to provide a sound basis for fiction in the increasingly complicated modern world, of which no satisfying personal overview could readily be obtained.

If we move from fiction to poetry in the decade 1910-20, we find an even greater emphasis on the need for new methods to convey the changing reality. The most vigorous statements of the need to make it new came from the young American Ezra Pound, a wonderfully exuberant denouncer of what he came to see—with encouragement from Ford—as the degeneracy of contemporary poetry: 'a horrible agglomerate compost, not minted, most of it not even baked, all legato, a doughy mess of second-hand Keats, Wordsworth, heaven knows what, fourth-hand Elizabethan sonority blunted, half-melted, lumpy.'[13] When Pound came to London in 1909 he soon met F.S. Flint and T.E. Hulme, both poets and critics with a similar distaste for the lack of discipline in contemporary poetry. Pound was apparently responsible for introducing the word 'Imagist' to describe the new style he was advocating, in which there would be directness and lucidity: 'Objective—no slither; direct—no excessive use of adjectives, no metaphors that won't permit examination.'[14] In *Poetry* (the Chicago magazine edited by Harriet Monroe for which Pound acted as foreign representative and which published a good deal of his poetry and criticism) in March 1913 the basic outlook of the group is described in 'Imagisme' by F.S. Flint and 'A Few Don'ts by an Imagist' by Pound (Nos. 5 and 10). Pound produced an anthology, *Des Imagistes* in 1914, and Amy Lowell (another energetic American poet, who came to London in 1915) brought out anthologies called *Some Imagist Poets* in 1915, 1916, and 1917, the first two with explanatory statements (No. 8). She included the young D.H. Lawrence among the contributors. But Pound found her taste in poetry lacking the necessary austerity, and protested that she had replaced Imagism by Amy-gism. The group soon fell apart. But it had administered a sharp critique of prevailing poetic practices which, in complex association with the grim effects of the Great War on the English sensibility, was to help to change English poetry in undeniable ways.

Some of the new ideas put forward by Pound are foreshadowed in the theory if not yet the practice of Yeats, the leading poet of the previous generation. In the series of short essays called 'Discoveries' which Yeats wrote in 1906-7 he discussed the effects on him of being involved in presenting drama to an uneducated audience in a small town in the West of Ireland. The experience led him to question the whole tradition to which his early work in both poetry and drama belonged, the tradition of romanticism and symbolism. The effect of this had been a subtle and sophisticated art, remote from the vocabulary and thought-processes of the Irish people, for whom it was nevertheless intended. In a section called 'Personality and the Intellectual Essences' Yeats notes that his involvement in the Irish theatre has faced him with the question, 'How can I make my work mean something to vigorous and simple men whose attention is not given to art but to a shop, or teaching in a National School, or dispensing medicine?'[15] He sees recent literature as having expressed only part of the human personality:

> In literature, partly from the lack of the spoken word which knits us to normal men, we have lost in personality, in our delight in the whole man–blood, imagination, intellect, running together–but have found a new delight, in essences, in states of mind, in pure imagination, in all that comes to us most easily in elaborate music.[16]

A choice has to be made by writers, either to go 'upward into ever-increasing subtlety' or 'downward, taking the soul with us until all is simplified and solidified again'[17] The latter course is clearly the one that now attracts Yeats, but he insists that it is not a matter of discarding the romantic 'soul', but rather of interjecting it into a new totality. This idea of poetry as an expression of 'the whole man' may be related to Eliot's view of the regrettable 'dissociation of sensibility' in his 1919 essay, 'The Metaphysical Poets' (No. 14). The stress on vigour and 'the tumult of the blood'[18] also relates Yeats to Pound and Lawrence.

The spirit of change was not confined to fiction and poetry; it affected the visual arts with equal force. The Post-Impressionist Exhibitions held at the Grafton Galleries in 1910 and 1912, which included work by Picasso, Matisse, Braque, and Derain, caused great controversy, making the English public aware, in the words of the art critic Roger Fry, writing in 1912, of 'a new movement in art, a movement which was the more disconcerting in that it was no mere variation upon accepted themes but implied a reconsideration of the very purpose and aim as well as the methods of pictorial and plastic art.'[19] Fry welcomed this new movement of artists who 'do not seek to imitate form, but to create form; not to imitate life, but to find an equivalent for life.'[20] It is notable that Fry describes the work of the French artists seen in the Exhibition as exhibiting a 'markedly classic spirit.'[21] He explains that he means by this that 'they do not rely for their effects upon associated ideas, as I believe Romantic and Realistic artists invariably do.'[22] English art seems to Fry to depend too much on associations, unlike the 'completely free and pure' art of Classicism which 'records a positive and disinterestedly passionate state of mind.'[23] The emphasis on disinterestedness is close to Stephen Dedalus in Joyce, while the employment of the term Classic suggests the ideas of T.E. Hulme, as expressed in *The New Age* and particularly in the essay 'Classicism and Romanticism' (No. 7).

In 1914 Fry's friend Clive Bell (Virginia Woolf's brother-in-law) published a book simply called *Art*, in which he asserted the importance of what he called 'significant form'–the formal relationships of lines and colours, which he claimed 'stir our aesthetic emotions' and which are therefore the defining characteristics of visual art. His formulation again takes the focus away from subject-matter onto form, and was evidently related, for all its anti-historicism, to a sympathetic response to contemporary art, especially in France, in its emphasis on 'simplification and design' rather than Impressionist concern with external reality.[24] Bell saw 'This passionate and austere art of the Contemporary Movement' as 'the inspiration, even the standard, of a young, violent and fierce generation.'[25] These qualities would certainly have appealed to Pound also, and he devoted much energy at this time to writing about painting and sculpture, partly as a result of meeting the young French sculptor, Henri Gaudier-Brzeska, in 1913. Pound's first piece on art, 'The New Sculpture' in the *Egoist* of 16 February 1914, was a celebration of the stylized art of Gaudier-Brzeska and Epstein. Gaudier-Brzeska fought in the War, and was killed on 5 June 1915 at Neuville St Vaast; Pound brought out a memorial volume in April 1916 including the sculptor's writings, photographs of his sculptures, and reproductions of his drawings. The magazine in which Gaudier-Brzeska had published his manifesto, 'Vortex', was the dramatically titled *BLAST*, edited by another aggressive artist and writer, Wyndham Lewis. Pound co-operated with Lewis in producing the first number of *BLAST* (No. 6); published in June 1914, it had a pink cover and employed large capitals and unusual typography to enforce its attitude on many aspects of English culture. The subtitle of the magazine, 'A Review of the Great English Vortex', promoted the name of the new approach as Vorticism, but the term never acquired wide currency; it did, however, suggest something of the ferocious energy valued by Lewis and expressed both in his paintings and his literary works, which include the novel *Tarr* (1918).

There is a striking contrast between the energetic iconoclasm of Lewis and Pound and the Brahmin elegance of the style in which T.S. Eliot formulated his literary principles, but there is no doubt of the continuity of their concerns. Eliot was to elaborate and develop ideas hastily promulgated by Pound, and so make them part of later academic criticism. But his ideas were as opposed as Pound's to the current poetic practice, just as the procedure of *Prufrock and Other Observations* in 1917 quietly undermined its conventions. *The Sacred Wood. Essays on Poetry and Criticism*, published in 1920, was an authoritative expression of the new outlook. It opens with a section entitled 'The Perfect Critic' in which Eliot sees English criticism as either vaguely abstract or vaguely impressionistic, contrasted with the rigour of Aristotle. Eliot's ideal, like Arnold's, is that of 'the disinterested exercise of intelligence'[26], exemplified in modern times for him by the French critic Rémy de Gourmont. Good criticism involves the forming of perceptions into structures, while bad criticism is 'nothing but an expression of emotion.'[27] Since this would also define bad poetry for Eliot, it can be seen how closely related are his views on criticism and his views on poetry. In both he sought the removal of 'the accident of personal emotion',[28] a formulation reminiscent of Flaubert's ideal of impersonality. These ideas are expressed more fully in the 1919 essay 'Tradition and the Individual Talent' (No. 13), which was to become perhaps the best-known statement of Eliot's position. Several of the other essays in the volume deal with the Jacobean drama, including 'Hamlet and his Problems' (1919) in which Eliot, in the course of a severe criticism of the play, propounds one of his best-known ideas, that of the 'objective correlative'. According to Eliot, *Hamlet* fails because Shakespeare is unable to treat the question of sexual guilt, raised in connection with Hamlet's attitude to his mother, in an open way; the play is 'full of some stuff that the writer could not drag to light, contemplate, or manipulate into art.'[29] The general idea which he draws from this is articulated thus:

> The only way of expressing emotion in the form of art is by finding an 'objective correlative'; in other words, a set of objects, a situation, a chain of events which shall be the formula of that *particular* emotion; such that when the external facts, which must terminate in sensory experience, are given, the emotion is immediately evoked.[30]

This emphatic statement contradicts the Romantic idea of poetry as the direct expression of emotion (as in Shelley's 'I fall upon the thorns of life, I bleed' in 'Ode to the West Wind'), and gives us the alternative Modernist idea of indirect expression through a dramatized object or situation which is in that way impersonal.

Joyce's *Ulysses* was first published serially in the *Little Review*, and the whole book in Paris in 1922. It rapidly became celebrated for its extraordinary techniques, arousing the hostility of conventional critics as much as the admiration of the more adventurous. Eliot's article in *The Dial* for November 1923 (No. 15) draws attention in particular to Joyce's use of Homer's *Odyssey*. It can be seen that in calling his own critical position 'classical'–which he did also in his editorials for the recently launched magazine *The Criterion*–Eliot was enforcing the ideal of impersonality discussed earlier. For him, Joyce's use of Homer is a valuable example of a new fictional method by which the writer can render contemporary experience. The traditional novel of narrative is felt to have ended with Flaubert and James, but 'Instead of narrative method, we may now use the mythical method'. This idea can be readily related to Eliot's own *The Waste Land*, which had appeared in 1922; it is less easy to relate it to much fiction after *Ulysses*. Novelists were perhaps more attached to 'narrative method' than Eliot realised, or were to depart from it by other means that the use of myth; the ideas of Lawrence and Woolf should be related to this formulation.

Eliot's next important critical work was *Homage to John Dryden* in 1924, which continued the criticism of the Romantics and the assertion of a new poetic. In 'The Metaphysical Poets' (No. 14) Eliot developed the idea of 'a dissociation of sensibility' in the English seventeenth century, which meant that thought and feeling were no longer unified as, it is suggested, was the case with Shakespeare and Donne. We may see here a parellel with Yeats's plea in 'Discoveries' for the bringing together of 'blood, imagination and intellect' (though 'blood' is not a quality with which Eliot shows much concern). The idea of the separation of thought and feeling, leading to Romantic and Victorian poetry in which the intellect plays an undesirably small part, is further elaborated in the essay 'Andrew Marvell'. Here the seventeenth-century poet is presented as having had the good fortune to write in the tradition of Ben Jonson, so that a characteristic poem of his, 'The Nymph Complaining for the Death of her Fawn', has a 'bright, hard precision', while a comparable Victorian poem, William Morris's 'The Nymph's Song to Hylas' is said to achieve its effect through 'the mistiness of the feeling and the vagueness of the object.'[31] Eliot generalizes the contrast to argue that nineteenth-century English poetry was largely occupied with the 'effort to construct a dream world'[32] and so rendered itself incapable of the 'wit' exemplified by Marvell, which Eliot calls 'this modest and certainly impersonal virtue...[which] is something precious and needed and apparently extinct.'[33] Eliot's own poetic practice involved the attempt to reintegrate the element of wit or, more broadly, intelligence into a discourse which had become, as all the Modernists felt, too exclusively emotional and personal.

By now our consideration has moved on to the 1920s when, as Malcolm Bradbury suggests, 'the *critical* revolution' developed, making more precise the implications of the insights of the radical practitioners of the previous decade. But there is in fact more overlap than his formulation implies, both in the case of Eliot and in those of Woolf and Lawrence, leading creative writers whose main critical essays appeared in the later decade. Virginia Woolf began writing as a novelist in the tradition of James with *The Voyage Out* (1915) and *Night and Day* (1919), but then felt the need to create a much freer form of fiction. Her 1919 essay 'Modern Fiction' (No. 16) expresses the innovatory viewpoint succinctly and effectively. The method is also appropriate, in that the imagery as well as the argument move the reader away from Victorian ideas of reality as solid and stable, towards a distinctively modern emphasis on instability and shapelessness, challenging the writer (and the reader) to create order out of this flux. 'Mr. Bennett and Mrs. Brown' (No. 17), given as a lecture in 1924, develops the criticism of the previous generation of novelists, described as Edwardians (Edward VII reigned from 1901 to 1910), along the lines suggested earlier by Ford and James. 'The Narrow Bridge of Art' of 1927 is also concerned with what was for Woolf the basic question of how writers can work efficiently in the modern atmosphere of 'doubt and conflict.'[34] These essays constitute the clearest statement of the Modernist view of fiction, and link the advocacy of it to a definite sense of overall social and cultural change.

Lawrence was another conscious innovator, in both poetry and fiction. Some of his early work was published by Ford in *The English Review*, and his poems appeared in *Some Imagist Poets* in 1915 and 1916. Pound remarked of him in a letter in 1913 that he had 'got to the point of the modern' before he [Pound] had, for all his efforts.[35] Nevertheless, Lawrence's views are as idiosyncratic as his style is vivid. He certainly shared the Modernist discontent with prevailing approaches, and this led him to move away from the basically realistic mode of his own early fiction up to *Sons and Lovers* (1913). As he began work on his next novel *The Sisters* (which eventually divided to become *The Rainbow* and *Women in Love*) in March 1913 he wrote to Edward Garnett, 'It is all analytical–quite unlike *Sons and Lovers*, not a bit visualized.'[36] The contrast between 'analytical' and 'visualized' suggests that Lawrence shares the Modernist ambition to go more deeply into his characters. But in what is probably his most famous letter, to Garnett, in June 1914, he expresses some agreement with the ideas of the Italian Futurist, Marinetti, who argued for a modern art relevant to the excitement of the Machine Age:

> Somehow–that which is physic–non-human, in humanity, is more interesting to me than the old-fashioned human element–which causes one to conceive a character in a certain moral scheme and make him consistent. The certain moral scheme is what I object to,[37]

Then Lawrence told Garnett not to expect a traditional novel of character:

> You mustn't look in my novel for the old stable *ego* of the character. There is another *ego*, according to whose action the individual is unrecognisable, and passes through, as it were, allotropic states which it needs a deeper sense than any we've been used to exercise, to discover are states of the same single radically unchanged element.[38]

This is a difficult idea, but it certainly suggests Lawrence's determination to explore character in a new way, seeking to show what lies below the personality projected in ordinary social life. This necessitated the new form of fiction which he was attempting to create, and which traditionally-minded critics saw as chaotic. Thus he wrote to his agent, J.B. Pinker, in 1916:

> Tell Arnold Bennett that all rules of construction hold good only for novels which are copies of other novels. A book which is not a copy of other books has its own construction, and what he calls faults, he being an old imitator, I call characteristics.[39]

But Lawrence's attitudes always have a strong moral element, and in 1912 he had written, 'I hate Bennett's resignation. Tragedy ought really to be a great kick at misery. But *Anna of the Five Towns* seems like an acceptance–so does all the modern stuff since Flaubert.'[40] Flaubert, we are told in the 1913 essay 'Thomas Mann', 'stood away from life as from a leprosy.'[41] Flaubert's 'standing away' is a kind of acceptance, but the new forms advocated by Lawrence are seen as making possible a more vivid and positive response to life, not simply a more aesthetically satisfying account of it. This is clear in his Preface to the *New Poems* published in New York in 1920 (No. 18), as well as in his pieces on the novel. These are all very general in their approach, and work by assertion rather than argument. 'Why the Novel Matters' (No. 21) asserts that the novel is the supreme form of human expression because it can get 'the whole hog' and does not have to simplify or dogmatise. 'Surgery for the Novel–or a Bomb?' (No. 19) criticises both the popular and the high-brow novel of the time. Perhaps literature can get back something of the thoughtfulness of Plato's dialogues; at all events it must break through to 'a new world outside'. Here and elsewhere Lawrence is grander and less technical than the other Modernists in his ambition. In 'Morality and the Novel' (No. 20) he again asserts the value of the novel, here related to its power to reveal the living relationship between man and 'the circumambient universe', both human and natural. If the novelist avoids didacticism, the novel can 'help us to live'; here again Lawrence's emphasis is more directly concerned with living than the pronouncements of the other Modernists. But his objection to the novelist who puts 'his thumb in the scale' to produce a simple moral statement may reasonably be seen as a form of the idea of artistic impersonality.

In 1919 Yeats published his 'A People's Theatre. A Letter to Lady Gregory' (No. 12). In it he deplored the fact that the success of the Abbey Theatre as an institution had been due to its preparedness to put on popular comedies rather than the kinds of traditional and mythological plays which he and Lady Gregory had originally hoped to offer to the Irish people. He refers to his own recently published

Mass culture (v) high culture ?

Four Plays for Dancers, written partly under the influence of the Japanese Noh plays, and wants to create 'an unpopular theatre and an audience like a secret society where admission is by favour and never to many'. This disillusioned but resolute argument may remind us of the striking fact that all the documents so far considered have referred to poetry and fiction, but not to drama. In the period covered by this anthology the drama seems to have been much less affected by new approaches than the other branches of literature. There were theatrical developments, like the Abbey Theatre itself or Granville Barker's work at the Royal Court Theatre, and controversial playwrights like Ibsen and Chekhov did make their way on the English stage. But there was no individual dramatist to lead a new school. Bernard Shaw, by far the most celebrated, although eloquent and innovative, was allied both by time and temperament with the generation of H.G. Wells, aiming to make the theatre a place of political and social debate. From the beginning Yeats had disliked Shaw's approach, seeing it as limited and limiting. He now believes the Abbey to have succumbed to similar tendencies. We may see his article as aspiring towards some kind of Modernist theatre, but he had neither the energy (in view of his commitment to poetry) nor the resources to create any such thing. There is no British equivalent of Bertolt Brecht.

As the 1920s passed, more exclusively critical writers can be seen alongside the practitioners. John Middleton Murry (1884-1957) had been publishing critical articles in the previous decade, but enjoyed increased scope as editor of *The Athenaeum* (1919-21) and founder of *The Adelphi* in 1923. His books consisted mainly of previously published articles: *Aspects of Literature* (1920), *Countries of the Mind* (1922), *Discoveries* (1924). In *Discoveries* Murry writes on 'The Significance of Russian Literature' and 'Anton Tchekov' (a now discarded transliteration of Chekhov), subjects also important to Virginia Woolf, and most interestingly in an essay on 'The Break-Up of the Novel' strangely discarded from subsequent editions. In it Murry discusses the achievement of Proust, Joyce and Dorothy Richardson, for all three of whom 'inner consciousness [is] reality'[42], but argues that this may lead fiction away into a total subjectivism which will leave the public behind. He argues instead in favour of the attempt 'to reconcile subjectivism with objectivity' which he terms 'the Tchekov tendency'[43], represented by the short-story writer (and Murry's wife) Katherine Mansfield (1888-1923), whose *Bliss and Other Stories* had appeared in 1920, *The Garden Party* in 1922, and *The Dove's Nest* in 1923. This is a kind of fiction in which there is some formal organisation for the reader to recognise and orientate himself by, 'an *art* which is compatible with truth'.[44] Murry raises the problem of the audience, which the demanding nature of Modernism makes problematic. This problem also concerns Richard Aldington in his *Studies and Reviews* of 1924.

But a good deal of the writing of the decade displayed the more detached tone which may be seen as marking the acceptance of Modernism and the beginnings of its academic study. Percy Lubbock in *The Craft of Fiction* (1921) gave a careful account of approaches to fiction, emphasising the idea of point-of-view so important to Henry James. I.A. Richards co-operated with C.K. Ogden to produce *The Foundations of Aesthetics* in 1922 and *The Meaning of Meaning* in 1923, before writing his *Principles of Literary Criticism* (1924), which employs a psychological approach which now seems over-simplified. However, the Appendix on 'The Poetry of T.S. Eliot' which Richards added to the second edition in 1926 (No. 22) shows his quality as a literary critic, and his *Practical Criticism* (1929), with its emphasis on the careful reading of untitled literary extracts, established one of the basic methods to be used in the expanding study of English literature. C.H. Rickword's 1926 'A Note on Fiction' (No. 23) is rightly said by Bradbury to be 'seminal...not only for *The Calendar* but for modern criticism generally, both in England and America. Many modern attitudes towards the criticism of fiction were concentrated in it.'[45] Rickword is urging an analytical approach and a more precise critical terminology. Edwin Muir (1887-1959) was to become a distinguished Scottish poet and, with his wife Willa, a translator of the works of Franz Kafka (1883-1924), the German-Czech Modernist. In *Transition: Essays on Contemporary Literature* (1926) the sureness of his judgment is suggested by the specific writers discussed, who include Joyce, Lawrence, Aldous Huxley, Woolf, Lytton Strachey, Eliot, Edith Sitwell and Robert Graves. The last chapter, on 'Contemporary Fiction', interestingly argues against the reductiveness he sees in these writers, which he regards as 'anti-humanistic.' He looks forward to a fiction which will 'humanize' 'the stuff on which Mr. Joyce works' by integrating it 'in human characters and in a complex of human life', and will 'set Mr. Bloom in motion, to place him in relation to figures as complex as himself'.[46] Muir's *The Structure of the Novel* (1928) discriminates between the novel of action, the novel of character, the dramatic novel and the chronicle, but is lacking in rigour by the standards of more recent criticism.

Herbert Read (1893-1968) was a poet and a prolific critic of both literature and art. His early books included *Reason and Romanticism*

(1926), *English Prose Style* (1928), *Phases of English Poetry* (1928) and *The Sense of Glory. Essays in Criticism* (1929). The last includes an essay on the eighteenth-century novelist Laurence Sterne–also admired by Virginia Woolf–which includes a perceptive comment about continuity in fiction:

> Continuity can be achieved in various ways, but in fiction we have in the past thought too exclusively of the continuity of action, of dramatic interest–in short, we have thought of a *mechanical* continuity. To that kind of continuity we nowadays oppose *psychological* continuity...Sterne is very modern in this sense. He is the precursor of all psychological fiction, which is as though we were to say: of all that is most significant in modern literature.[47]

In 1927 E.M. Forster published his Clark Lectures as *Aspects of the Novel*. The tone of the writing shows Forster playing the part of a successful novelist–*A Passage to India* had appeared in 1924–who is not going to surrender to an academic atmosphere. Hence the suggestion that Percy Lubbock is being over-technical in his discussion of the novelist and point-of-view, while what matters is simply 'the power of the writer to bounce the reader into accepting what he says...the novelist must bounce us; that is imperative'.[48] Forster has some difficulty in combining his casualness with the attempt to introduce some critical terms such as fantasy, prophecy, pattern and rhythm, and the much-quoted distinction between round and flat characters remains very inexact. But no-one has better stated the ambivalence of the Modernist novelist towards the narrative element, which may be felt to form the basis of his art, than Forster in this wry remark:

> Yes–oh dear yes–the novel tells a story. This is the fundamental aspect without which it could not exist. That is the highest common factor of all novels, and I wish that it was not so, that it could be something different–melody, or perception of the truth, not this low atavistic form.

The year 1927 also saw the publication of *A Survey of Modernist Poetry* by the two poets Laura Riding and Robert Graves. Their lively book includes an excellent formulation of the Modernist attitude to form:

> The whole trend of modern poetry is toward treating poetry like a sensitive substance which succeeds better when allowed to crystallize by itself than when put into prepared moulds...Modern poetry, that is, is groping for some principle of self-determination to be applied to the making of the poem–not lack of government, but government from within.[50]

In terms of this definition, the subtle unity of *The Waste Land* is contrasted with the purely artificial unity of form of Tennyson's *In Memoriam*.[51] The book is marked throughout by the 'intelligent ease'[52] which it ascribes to the Modernist approach.

When in 1928 Eliot produced a second edition of *The Sacred Wood*, he noted in the Preface that 'many important books of critical theory and practice' had appeared since its original publication in 1920. This anthology has attempted to represent or discuss the work referred to. Eliot then remarked that in 1920, under the influence of Rémy de Gourmont, he had been concerned mainly with 'the problem of the integrity of poetry', but that now in 1928 he was conscious of passing on to another problem, 'that of the relation of poetry to the spiritual and social life of its time and other times.'[54] That new preoccupation points us away from the central concerns of the Modernists towards the greater political and social emphasis of the succeeding decade.

Modernism had achieved its major innovations by 1930, the date at which this anthology ends, although major works by Eliot, Joyce, Pound and Woolf were still to come, and its influence was to remain powerful up to our own day. In general it had come to be accepted by those who took the arts seriously as having produced great results, even if at the cost of seriously distancing art from many people. It was left to the Hungarian Marxist, Georg Lukács, to make the most outright assault on it, especially in 'The Ideology of Modernism' in 1955. It is the subjectivism which Lukács sees in Modernist art which appalls him in Kafka, Joyce, Faulkner, Beckett and Eliot:

> Kafka's artistic ingenuity is really directed towards substituting his *angst*-ridden vision of the world for objective reality... A similar attenuation of reality underlies Joyce's stream of consciousness... Man is reduced to a sequence of unrelated fragments; he is as inexplicable to others as to himself.[55]

Lukács goes on to argue that Modernism shares with Naturalism (the method of Zola, with which it is often contrasted) 'a basically static approach to reality'.[56] The approach which shows the dynamic or dialectical nature of human history is Realism, the method of nineteenth-century fiction carried on into the twentieth by the Russian Gorky and the German Thomas Mann. This method fuses the particular and the general, whereas Modernism offers only the particular. For Lukács it means therefore 'not the enrichment but the negation of art'.[57] Important issues are raised here, and the debate is not likely to be easily settled. Other Marxists have taken a very different attitude: Bertolt Brecht's work in the theatre led to the creation of what we may regard as Modernist drama, and the critic Walter Benjamin was to write favourably and subtly in *Illuminations* (1955) of Kafka, Brecht and Proust.

The discussion of Modernism has by this time produced a large amount of critical writing, some of which is recommended for further reading at the end of this book. David Lodge's essay 'Modernism, Antimodernism, and Postmodernism' in *Working with Structuralism* (1981) suggests some of the terminology which has developed for the consideration of more recent developments. But this anthology will have succeeded if it has helped to increase awareness of the complex critical thinking which was so important a part of the development of Modernism in England in the early twentieth century, and whose full implications, if thoroughly understood, might still enrich today's confident theorizing.

Notes

1   Stephen Spender, *The Struggle of the Modern* (1963), p.71.
2   Malcolm Bradbury, Introduction to *The Calendar of Modern Letters*, I (1966), vii-viii.
3   Joyce, *Stephen Hero* (1969), p.103.
4   ibid. p.216.
5   'Flaubert, 1893' in M. Shapira, ed., *Henry James, Selected Literary Criticism* (1963), p.173.
6   'Flaubert, 1902' in ibid. p.262.
7   James, *The Portrait of a Lady*, ed. N. Bradbury (1981), p.xxx
8   Ford, *The Critical Attitude* (1911), p.110.
9   L. Edel and G. Rays, eds., *Henry James and H. G. Wells* (1958), pp.137-8.
10   ibid. p.148.
11   ibid. p.154.
12   ibid. p.156.
13   Quoted in P. Jones, ed., *Imagist Poetry* (1972), p.14.
14   See P. Jones, ed., *Imagist Poetry* (1972), Introduction, p.17.
15   W.B. Yeats, *Essays* (1924), p.325.
16   ibid. p.330.
17   ibid. p.330.
18   ibid. p.331.
19   Roger Fry, 'Preface' to 'Catalogue of the Second Post-Impressionist Exhibition' of 1912, in *Vision and Design* (1920; 1928), p.237.
20   ibid. p.239.
21   ibid. p.241.
22   ibid. pp.211-12.
23   ibid. p.242.
24   Clive Bell, *Art* (1914; 1928), pp.215-38.
25   ibid. p.244.
26   T.S. Eliot, *The Sacred Wood* (1920), p.12.
27   ibid. p.15.
28   ibid.

29   ibid. p.100.
30   ibid.
31   Eliot, *Homage to John Dryden* (1924), p.299.
32   ibid. p.301.
33   ibid. p.304.
34   Woolf, *Collected Essays*, II (1966/7), p.219.
35   D.D. Paige, ed., *The Letters of Ezra Pound: 1907-41* (New York, 1950), p.52.
36   A. Beal, ed., *D.H. Lawrence. Selected Literary Criticism* (1956), p.14.
37   ibid. p.17.
38   ibid. p.18.
39   ibid. p.20.
40   ibid. p.131.
41   ibid. p.265.
42   Murry, 'The Break-Up of the Novel' in *Discoveries* (1924), p.140.
43   ibid. p.141.
44   ibid. p.144.
45   Bradbury, op.cit. p.xviii.
46   Edwin Muir, *Transition. Essays on Contemporary Literature* (1926), p.217.
47   Herbert Read, 'Sterne' in *Collected Essays in Literary Criticism* (1928; 1976), p.264.
48   E.M. Forster, *Aspects of the Novel* (1927; 1976), p.82.
49   ibid. p.40.
50   Laura Riding and Robert Graves, *A Survey of Modernist Poetry* (1927; 1929), p.47.
51   ibid. p.51.
52   ibid. p.179.
53   T.S. Eliot, *The Sacred Wood* 2nd Edition (1928), p.viii.
54   ibid. p.viii.
55   G. Lukács, 'The Ideology of Modernism' in *The Meaning of Contemporary Realism* (1957; English translation 1963), p.26.
56   ibid. p.35.
57   ibid. p.46.

A Modernist Reader

Henry James

James (1843-1916) was the leading theorist of fiction in England in the early twentieth century. His most recent novels were The Wings of The Dove *(1902),* The Ambassadors *(1903) and* The Golden Bowl *(1904). His critical work included* French Poets and Novelists *(1878),* Partial Portraits *(1888),* Essays in London and Elsewhere *(1893), the series of Prefaces to the New York edition of his novels (1907-8), and* Notes on Novelists *(1914).*

Leon Edel edited Selected Letters of Henry James *in 1956, and Morris Shapira edited the useful* Henry James. Selected Literary Criticism *in 1963, which includes 'The New Novel'.*

1 From a letter to Hugh Walpole,[1] 13 May 1910

I 'read', in a manner, 'Maradick'[2]–but there's too much to say about it, and even my weakness doesn't alter me from the grim and battered old *critical* critic–no *other* such creature among all the 'reviewers' do I meanwhile behold. Your book has a geat sense and love of life–but seems to me very nearly as irreflectively juvenile as the Trojans,[3] and to have the prime defect of your having gone into a subject–i.e. the marital, sexual, bedroom relations of M. and his wife–the literary man and his wife–since these *are* the key to the whole situation–which have to be tackled and faced to mean anything. You don't tackle and face them–you *can't*. Also the whole thing is a monument to the abuse of voluminous dialogue, the absence of a plan of composition, alternation, distribution, structure, and other phases of presentation than the dialogue–so that *line* (the only thing *I* value in a fiction etc.) is replaced by a vast formless featherbediness–billows in which one sinks and is lost. And yet it's all so loveable–though not so *written*. It isn't written *at all*, darling Hugh–by which I mean you have–or, truly, only in a few places, as in Maradick's dive–never got expression *tight* and in close quarters (of discrimination, of specification) with its subject. It remains loose and far. And you have never made out, recognised, nor stuck to, the *centre of your subject*. But can you forgive all this to your fondest old reaching-out-his-arms-to-you.   H.J.

1 Walpole (1884-1941) was a young novelist with whom James was on friendly terms, but whose novels distressed him by their lack of form.
2 *Maradick at Forty* had been published in April 1910.
3 *The Wooden Horse* was Walpole's previous novel, published in 1909.

2 From a letter to Walpole, 19 May 1912

I rejoice in the getting on of your work–how splendidly copious your flow; and am much interested in what you tell me of your readings and your literary emotions. These latter indeed–or some of them, as you express them, I don't think I fully share. At least when you ask me if I don't feel Dostoieffsky's[1] 'mad jumble, that flings things down in a heap', nearer truth and beauty than the picking and composing that you instance in Stevenson,[2] I reply with emphasis that I feel nothing of the sort, and that the older I grow and the more I *go* the more sacred to me do picking and composing become–though I naturally don't limit myself to Stevenson's *kind* of the same. Don't let anyone persuade you–there are plenty of ignorant and fatuous duffers to try to do it–that strenuous selection and comparison are not the very essence of art, and that Form *is* [not] substance to that degree that there is absolutely no substance without it. Form alone *takes*, and holds and preserves, substance–saves it from the welter of helpless verbiage that we swim in as in a sea of tasteless tepid pudding, and that makes one ashamed of an art capable of such degradations. Tolstoi and D. are fluid pudding, though not tasteless, because the amount of their own minds and souls in solution in the broth gives it savour and flavour, thanks to the strong, rank quality of their genius and their experience. But there are all sorts of things to be said of them, and in particular that we see how great a vice is their lack of composition, their defiance of economy and architecture, directly they are emulated and imitated; *then*, as subjects of emulation, models, they quite give themselves away. There is nothing so deplorable as a work of art with a *leak* in its interest; and there is no such leak of interest as through commonness of form. Its opposite, the *found* (because the sought-for,) form is the absolute citadel and tabernacle of interest. But what a lecture I am reading you–though a very imperfect one–which you have drawn upon yourself (as moreover it was quite right you should.) But no matter–I shall go for you again–as soon as I find you in a lone corner.

1 Fyodor Dostoievsky (1821-81) became known in England at the time through the translations of Constance Garnett; that of *The Brothers Karamazov* in 1912 was particularly well received; see G. Phelps, *The Russian Novel in English Fiction* (1956), p.15.

2   Robert Louis Stevenson (1850-94), though best-known for his adventure story *Treasure Island* (1883), was a serious novelist with an interest in French ideas on fictional technique.

3   From 'The New Novel', 1914

This was·originally published in the Times Literary Supplement *635 (10 March 1914), 133-4 and 637 (2 April 1914), 157-8, as 'The Younger Generation'. It was revised and retitled for inclusion in* Notes on Novelists *(1914).*

The article discusses recent novels by Gilbert Cannan, D.H. Lawrence, Compton Mackenzie and Hugh Walpole, who are all seen as being influenced in their methods by the two leading Edwardian novelists, Arnold Bennett (1867-1931) and H.G. Wells (1866-1946). Bennett had published Clayhanger *in 1910, and was known as the chronicler of the life of the Five Towns of the Staffordshire potteries; Wells had published* Tono-Bungay *in 1909 and* The New Machiavelli *in 1911.*

Mr Wells and Mr Arnold Bennett (speaking now only of them) began some time back to show us, and to show sundry emulous and generous young spirits then in the act of more or less waking up, what the state in question might amount to. We confound the author of *Tono-Bungay* and the author of *Clayhanger* in this imputation for the simple reason that with the sharpest differences of character and range they yet come together under our so convenient measure of value by *saturation*. This is the greatest value, to our sense, in either of them, their other values, even when at the highest, not being quite in proportion to it; and as to be documented, to be able even on occasion to prove quite enviably and potently so, they are alike in the authority that creates emulation. It little signifies that Mr Wells's documented or saturated state in respect to a particular matter in hand is but one of the faces of his *generally* informed condition, of his extraordinary mass of gathered and assimilated knowledge, a miscellaneous collection more remarkable surely than any teller of 'mere' tales, with the possible exception of Balzac,[1] has been able to draw upon, whereas Mr Arnold Bennett's corresponding provision affects us as, though singularly copious, special, exclusive and artfully economic. This distinction avails nothing against that happy fact of the handiest possession by Mr Wells of immeasurably more concrete material, amenable for straight and vivid reference, convertible into apt illustration, than we should know where to look for examples of. The author of *The New Machiavelli* knows, somehow, to our mystified and dazzled apprehension, because he writes and because that act constitutes for him the need, on occasion a most desperate one, of absorbing knowledge at the pores; the chronicler of the *Five Towns* writing so much more discernibly, on the other hand, because he knows, and conscious of no need more desperate than that particular circle of civilization may satisfy.

Our argument is that each is ideally immersed in his own body of reference, and that immersion in any such degree and to the effect of any such variety, intensity and plausibility is really among us a new feature of the novelist's range of resource.

[...] Nothing is further from our thought than to undervalue saturation and possession, the fact of the particular experience, the state and degree of acquaintance incurred, however such a consciousness may have been determined; for these things represent on the part of the novelist, as on the part of any painter of things seen, felt or imagined, just one half of his authority—the other half being represented of course by the application he is inspired to make of them. Therefore that fine secured half is so much gained at the start, and the fact of its brightly being there may really by itself project upon the course so much colour and form as to make us on occasion, under the genial force, almost not miss the answer to the question of application. When the author of *Clayhanger* has put down upon the table, in dense unconfused array, every fact required, every fact in any way invocable, to make the life of the *Five Towns* press upon us, and to make our sense of it, so full-fed, content us, we may very well go on for the time in the captive condition, the beguiled and bemused condition, the acknowledgement of which is in general our highest tribute to the temporary master of our sensibility. Nothing at such moments—or rather at the end of them, when the end begins to threaten—may be of a more curious strain than the dawning unrest that suggests to us fairly our first critical comment: 'Yes, yes—but is this *all?* These are the circumstances of the interest—we see, we see; but where is the interest itself, where and what is its centre, and how are we to measure it in relation to *that?*'

1 Honoré de Balzac (1799-1850), the French novelist whose *Comédie Humaine* attempted to give a realistic account of a whole society.

Ford Madox Ford

Ford (1873-1939)–known as Hueffer until 1919–founded and edited The
English Review *(1908-9). He had co-operated with Conrad in writing*
Romance *(1903), and was a keen advocate of new methods in both fiction
and poetry. His best novels were to be* The Good Soldier *(1915),* Some Do
Not *(1924),* No More Parades *(1925),* A Man Could Stand Up *(1926)*
and Last Post *(1928), the last four concerning the Great War, in which Ford*
fought.

4 *From* The Critical Attitude *(1911)*

These sections from Chapter IV 'English Literature of Today' (pp.88-93;
107) had originally been published in The English Review *for November*
1909 under the title 'The Critical Attitude'.

We have amongst us, at the present time, perhaps some six purely
imaginative writers whose work it may be here profitable to study in
the effort to discover whether there exists any school of conscious
Literary Art in England today. For ostensibly there is nothing but a
formless welter of books without any tendency as without any
traditions or aesthetic aims. Of these six writers three–Mr Henry
James, Mr Joseph Conrad[1] and Mr George Moore[2]–we may regard as
being wholly concerned with their Art, as belonging to the School
which represents the mainstream of the current of European
Literature, and as having no external considerations for anything but
their individual presentations of life. We have Mr Galsworthy,[3] whom
we may regard as belonging technically to the same school, but as
falling short of ultimate preoccupation with his Art. And we have two
imaginative writers who, not artists in the strict sense that they have
any canons of Art by which they work, yet by virtue of personalities
attractive or unusual, carry on in the typically English manner the
traditions of the insularly English novel. These are Mr H.G. Wells
and Mr Rudyard Kipling.[4] These writers do not, of course, exhaust
the catalogue of novelists whose work is worthy of attention or perusal,

but they stand out as very excellent signposts to mark the difference between the more insular and amateur and the more cosmopolitan and scientific schools of writers at present at work in these kingdoms.

Mr Conrad and Mr James stand so far above any other imaginative writers of today, that their significance and their importance are apt to be a little lost. They stand, moreover, so far apart one from another that they have, as far as any literary movement is concerned, an entire want of unity or cohesion. They are united by one thing–by an extreme literary conscientiousness. With personalities so absolutely differing that the fact is obscured, the literary methods of each are in essentials the same. Each takes in hand an 'affair'–a parcel of life, that is to say, in which several human beings are involved–and each having taken hold never loosens his grip until all that can possibly be extracted from the human situation is squeezed out. The defect of each as an artist is his too close engrossment in the affair he has in hand. In each case this leads to what is called digressions. Mr James digresses because he desires to build up round his figures an immense atmosphere of the complexities of relationships. He loses hold, from time to time, of the faculty of selection; he will step aside to introduce some subtlety of relationship because it is quaint or because it amuses him; he will neglect to observe that this subtlety does not help his story forward and that thus he has gone outside his mainstream. Mr Conrad is much less concerned with spiritual relationships and much more with a sort of material fatalism. For him every one of the situations of a book must be rendered inevitable. The actual situations thus set up he is less careful to define. In that way he is an impressionist. If he had to describe, let us say, a murder, he would give his story the true tragic note. The motive for the murder would be overwhelming, the circumstances in which it was brought about would be so described that we should imagine ourselves to be present at the actual time. But not only this, Mr Conrad would find it necessary to describe minutely the knife with which the murder was committed, the manner in which it fitted into the murderer's hand. Nay, more; supposing the murderer to be an individual of a wild or an excited appearance, Mr Conrad's conscience would make it necessary that he should minutely describe the man who sold the murderer the knife. He might provide us with the genealogy of the seller in order to prove that owing to the idiosyncrasies of his father and mother he was predisposed to the selling of lethal instruments to men of wild appearance. Or he might give us an account of the vendor's financial ups and downs for the preceding two years in order absolutely to convince us that the vendor was inevitably forced by destiny to dispose of the knife. In the former case the cap of the vendor's mother and the photographs over her parlour mantelpiece would be carefully described in order to render *her* real; in the latter, the knife-seller's account-books would be sedulously projected before us, and at the moment when he was hesitating whether or not to sell the knife there would float before his eyes, written in red ink, the amount of the balance against him at his bank. But these digressions, if they serve to take up time, do give to Mr Conrad's work its extraordinary aspect of reality. Without them we we should not feel that we are experiencing–at least to the extent that Mr Conrad would experience them–the actual scenes that he describes for us. Without them, indeed, it is very likely that Mr Conrad's impressionism would fail of its effect. For having minutely described the purchase of the dagger, Mr Conrad would go on to render for us the journey of the murderer in a four-wheeler through a thick fog. We should be conducted to the door of a house where the crime was to be committed, the rust of the knocker would be felt, not seen, because of the thickness of the fog. The door would open upon a black hall and there the episode would end. The point would be that Mr Conrad would by this time so entirely have identified us with the spirit of the expedition that we should take up the tale for ourselves. We should go up the creaking stairs which Mr Conrad beforehand would have described for us with such intimacy that we should feel ourselves simply at home; we should push open the door and in the shadow of the bed-curtains we should perceive a sleeping form. But Mr Conrad, having dropped his story with the knocker upon the front door, would begin his next chapter with an observation from Inspector Frost, of the Secret Service. He would describe the room in which Inspector Frost sat and he would give us the inspector's biography, with an episode of his school life which would go to prove how inevitable it was that the inspector should pass his days in the detection of crime. And so once more Mr Conrad would take up the story of the murder with the inspector's description in colloquial English of what the corpse's hands looked like.

But it is to be observed that any faults at all cardinal in the writings of these two great artists arise from nothing but their too great attention to their Art. Their defects, in short, are those of over-consciousness. It may be observed that both Mr Conrad and Mr James are somewhat limited in the range of life which they treat. But that again is a form of conscientiousness, since a writer can only really write with assurance of the life which he himself has lived. And it is the characteristic of both these writers–who were trained in the same school–that they are unable to write with any pretended feeling of assurance of the planes of life with which they are unacquainted. They are, that is to say, in the strictest sense, realists, whether they treat of the romantic and the far away or of the everyday and the here.

Both Mr James and Mr Conrad are products of the great French school of writers of the eighties. They are thus in the main-stream of that development of modern Literature which, beginning with Richardson,[5] crossed the Channel to influence Diderot[6] (we are thinking of his *Rameau's Nephew*), and the Encyclopædists, to issue, as it were, by means of Chateaubriand[7] into that wonderful group whose fervour for their Art drew together Flaubert,[8] Maupassant,[9] Turgenev,[10] the Goncourts[11] and the rest. Mr James is, as it were, more essentially the child of Turgenev, Mr Conrad draws his blood more widely from the whole group, but it is safe to say that had these writers not existed, neither Mr James nor Mr Conrad would have written at all as they do. There remains one other very distinguished exponent of this school whom we have left unmentioned – Mr George Moore. Mr Moore once delivered himself of the witticism: 'Mr James came to Europe and studied Turgenev. Mr Howells[12] remained in America and studied Mr Henry James.' Mr George Moore, on the other hand, left Dublin to study Guy de Maupassant. And so closely has he assimilated the technical methods of the author of *Une Vie* that, except for the language, *Esther Waters* or *Evelyn Innes* have nothing to show that they did not emanate from the pen that wrote *La Maison Tellier*.

We have treated, of course, only of the writers who are typical of certain movements – of those whom it is possible to classify. For outside the ranks of these two literary schools there remain an infinite number of novelists producing, some of them, work eminently creditable with or without knowledge of what they are actually achieving. And there are, we are well aware, several younger writers whose output, though it has hitherto been limited, has yet maintained a very high level of conscience. But it is obvious that we could do no more than we have done. Our task has been rather to discover whether there did or did not exist in England a school of Literature at all, or whether Literature of today was all and altogether a matter of disunited and disordered individual activities without tendencies as without traditions, without standards as without aspirations. And we think we have proved that, in the case of such writers as Mr James, Mr Conrad and Mr George Moore, the great main-stream of European International Literature is cultivating still in England the muses upon a little thin oatmeal. The temperamentally British novel, the loose, amorphous, genial and easy-going thing that was represented by

Fielding, by Dickens and by Thackeray, and with more art and less geniality by Anthony Trollope–this thing that is as essentially national as is the English pudding–is a little more difficult to discern. But Mr Wells has his spiritual kinship with Dickens: Mr Kipling is, or perhaps we should say was, a less discursive Thackeray. And have we not Mr. William de Morgan?[13]

1   Conrad (1857-1924), the Polish novelist who had settled in England, had most recently published *The Secret Agent* (1907).
2   Moore (1852-1933) was an Irish novelist and admirer of the French tradition; he published *Esther Waters* in 1894 and *Evelyn Innes* in 1896.
3   John Galsworthy (1867-1933) was known for the social and political concerns expressed in his plays *Strife* (1909) and *Justice* (1910), and his novels *The Man of Property* (1906) and *Fraternity* (1909).
4   Kipling (1865-1936) had published numerous books of prose and verse including *Kim* (1901), *Puck of Pook's Hill* (1906) and *Rewards and Fairies* (1910).
5   Samuel Richardson (1689-1761), author of *Pamela* (1740-1) and *Clarissa Harlowe* (1747-8).
6   Denis Diderot (1713-84), one of the founders of the *Encylopédie*, wrote *Le Neveu de Rameau* some time in the 1770s; it was not published in his lifetime.
7   René de Chateaubriand (1768-1848), a pioneer of romanticism in France, especially in the autobiographical *René* (1802).
8   Gustave Flaubert (1821-80), author of *Madame Bovary* (1857) and *L'Education Sentimentale* (1869).
9   Guy de Maupassant (1850-93) published *La Maison Tellier* in 1881 and *Une Vie* in 1883.
10   Ivan Turgenev (1818-83), the Russian author of *On the Eve* (1860) and *Fathers and Sons* (1862).
11   The Goncourts: Edmond de Goncourt (1822-92) and his brother Jules (1830-70) published together the novels *Germinie Lacerteux* (1864) and *Madame Gervaisais* (1869).
12   William Dean Howells (1837-1920), American novelist, author of *The Rise of Silas Lapham* (1885).
13   William de Morgan (1839-1917) was a fine potter and tile-maker, who turned to writing fiction with *Joseph Vance* (1906) and *An Affair of Dishonour* (1909).

F.S. Flint

Frank Stuart Flint (1885-1960) was a self-educated poet and critic with a special interest in French literature. He contributed regularly to The Poetry Review *(later renamed* Poetry and Drama*), including the important long article 'Contemporary French Poetry' in* The Poetry Review *I, 8 (1912), 355-414. He became associated with Hulme, Pound, and the Imagist movement, though his relationship with Pound was stormy; see Christopher Middleton, 'Documents on Imagism from the Papers of F.S. Flint' in* The Review *15 (April 1965), 35-51. He published his own 'History of Imagisme' in* The Egoist *II, 5 (1 May 1915), 70-1.*

He is well represented in Peter Jones's useful Imagist Poetry *(1972).*

5 'Imagisme'; from Poetry *(Chicago) I, 6 (March 1913).*
The Editor's Note reads:

> ... In response to many requests for information regarding *Imagism* and the *Imagistes*, we publish this note by Mr. Flint, supplementing it with further exemplification by Mr. Pound. It will be seen from these that *Imagism* is not necessarily associated with Hellenic subjects, or with *vers libre* as a prescribed form.

The Imagiste *with whom Flint discussed the movement was evidently Ezra Pound; Middleton, in 'Documents on Imagism' referred to above, includes a transcription of a typescript headed 'Les Imagistes. A Note and an Interview by F.S. Flint' which shows Pound's amendments to Flint's original (pp.36-8). The 'further exemplification by Mr. Pound' consisted of 'A Few Don'ts by An Imagiste', included in the present volume in Pound's 'A Retrospect', pp.60-63.*

Some curiosity has been aroused concerning *Imagisme*, and as I was unable to find anything definite about it in print, I sought out an *imagiste*, with intent to discover whether the group itself knew anything about the 'movement.' I gleaned these facts.

The *Imagistes* admitted that they were contemporaries of the Post

40

Impressionists and the Futurists; but they had nothing in common with these schools. They had not published a manifesto. They were not a revolutionary school; their only endeavour was to write in accordance with the best tradition, as they found it in the best writers of all time,–in Sappho,[1] Catullus,[2] Villon.[3] They seemed to be absolutely intolerant of all poetry that was not written in such endeavour, ignorance of the best tradition forming no excuse. They had a few rules, drawn up for their own satisfaction only, and they had not published them. They were:

1. Direct treatment of the 'thing', whether subjective or objective.
2. To use absolutely no word that did not contribute to the presentation.
3. As regarding rhythm: to compose in sequence of the musical phrase, not in sequence of a metronome.

By these standards they judged all poetry, and found most of it wanting. They held also a certain 'Doctrine of the Image', which they had not committed to writing; they said that it did not concern the public, and would provoke useless discussion.

The devices whereby they persuaded approaching poetasters to attend their instruction were:

1. They showed him his own thought already splendidly expressed in some classic (and the school musters altogether a most formidable erudition).
2. They re-wrote his verses before his eyes, using about ten words to his fifty.

Even their opponents admit of them–ruefully–'At least they do keep bad poets from writing!'

I found among them an earnestness that is amazing to one accustomed to the usual London air of poetic dilettantism. They consider that Art is all science, all religion, philosophy and metaphysic. It is true that *snobisme* may be urged against them; but it is at least *snobisme* in its most dynamic form, with a great deal of sound sense and energy behind it; and they are stricter with themselves than with any outsider.

1 Greek lyric poet of the seventh century BC
2 Gaius Valerius Catullus (*c*.84-*c*.54 BC), Roman poet.
3 François Villon, French poet of the fifteenth century.

Wyndham Lewis

Percy Wyndham Lewis (1884-1957) came to England from America as a child, and later studied at the Slade School of Art. He was a powerful advocate of new methods in art and literature, using the term 'Vorticism' to evoke the desired spirit of energy and abstraction. His novel Tarr *was published in 1918, and his autobiographical* Blasting and Bombardiering *in 1937.*

Walter Michel and C.J. Fox edited Wyndham Lewis on Art *in 1969, which includes* BLAST.

6 From BLAST. The Review of the Great English Vortex *1, (1914).*

The aggressive typography and literary style emphasise Lewis's determination to attack old values and assert the new: to preserve the distinctive flavour of the original it is reproduced here in facsimile. Lewis joined the artillery in the Great War, and had to discontinue the magazine after its second number in 1915.

Long Live the Vortex!

Long live the great art vortex sprung up in the centre of this town !

We stand for the Reality of the Present—not for the sentimental Future, or the sacripant Past.

We want to leave Nature and Men alone.

We do not want to make people wear Futurist Patches, or fuss men to take to pink and sky-blue trousers.

We are not their wives or tailors.

The only way Humanity can help artists is to remain independent and work unconsciously.

WE NEED THE UNCONSCIOUSNESS OF HUMANITY—their stupidity, animalism and dreams.

We believe in no perfectibility except our own.

Intrinsic beauty is in the Interpreter and Seer, not in the object or content.

We do not want to change the appearance of the world, because we are not Naturalists, Impressionists or Futurists (the latest form of Impressionism), and do not depend on the appearance of the world for our art.

WE ONLY WANT THE WORLD TO LIVE, and to feel it's crude energy flowing through us.

It may be said that great artists in England are always revolutionary, just as in France any really fine artist had a strong traditional vein.

Blast sets out to be an avenue for all those vivid and violent ideas that could reach the Public in no other way.

Blast will be popular, essentially. It will not appeal to any particular class, but to the fundamental and popular instincts in every class and description of people, TO THE INDIVIDUAL. The moment a man feels or realizes himself as an artist, he ceases to belong to any milieu or time. Blast is created for this timeless, fundamental Artist that exists in everybody.

The Man in the Street and the Gentleman are equally ignored.

Popular art does not mean the art of the poor people, as it is usually supposed to. It means the art of the individuals.

Education (art education and general education) tends to destroy the creative instinct. Therefore it is in times when education has been non-existant that art chiefly flourished.

But it is nothing to do with " the People."

It is a mere accident that that is the most favourable time for the individual to appear.

To make the rich of the community shed their education skin, to destroy polite-ness, standardization and academic, that is civilized, vision, is the task we have set ourselves.

We want to make in England not a popular art, not a revival of lost folk art, or a romantic fostering of such unactual conditions, but to make individuals, wherever found.

We will convert the King if possible.

A VORTICIST KING ! WHY NOT?

DO YOU THINK LLOYD GEORGE HAS THE VORTEX IN HIM ?

MAY WE HOPE FOR ART FROM LADY MOND ?

We are against the glorification of " the People," as we are against snobbery. It is not necessary to be an outcast bohemian, to be unkempt or poor, any more than it is necessary to be rich or handsome, to be an artist. Art is nothing to do with the coat you wear. A top-hat can well hold the Sixtine. A cheap cap could hide the image of Kephren.

AUTOMOBILISM (Marinetteism) bores us. We don't want to go about making a hullo-bulloo about motor cars, anymore than about knives and forks, elephants or gas-pipes.

Elephants are VERY BIG. Motor cars go quickly.

Wilde gushed twenty years ago about the beauty of machinery. Gissing, in his romantic delight with modern lodging houses was futurist in this sense.

The futurist is a sensational and sentimental mixture of the aesthete of 1890 and the realist of 1870.

The " Poor " are detestable animals ! They are only picturesque and amusing for the sentimentalist or the romantic ! The " Rich " are bores without a single exception, *en tant que riches !*

We want those simple and great people found everywhere.

Blast presents an art of Individuals.

OUR VORTEX.

I.

Our vortex is not afraid of the Past : it has forgotten it's existence.

Our vortex regards the Future as as sentimental as the Past.

The Future is distant, like the Past, and therefore sentimental.

The mere element " Past " must be retained to sponge up and absorb our melancholy.

Everything absent, remote, requiring projection in the veiled weakness of the mind, is sentimental.

The Present can be intensely sentimental—especially if you exclude the mere element " Past."

Our vortex does not deal in reactive Action only, nor identify the Present with numbing displays of vitality.

The new vortex plunges to the heart of the Present.

The chemistry of the Present is different to that of the Past. With this different chemistry we produce a New Living Abstraction.

The Rembrandt Vortex swamped the Netherlands with a flood of dreaming.

The Turner Vortex rushed at Europe with a wave of light.

We wish the Past and Future with us, the Past to mop up our melancholy, the Future to absorb our troublesome optimism.

With our Vortex the Present is the only active thing.

Life is the Past and the Future.

The Present is Art.

II.

Our Vortex insists on water—tight compartments.

There is no Present—there is Past and Future, and there is Art.

Any moment not weakly relaxed and slipped back, or, on the other hand, dreaming optimistically, is Art.

" Just Life " or soi-disant " Reality " is a fourth quantity, made up of the Past, the Future and Art.

This impure Present our Vortex despises and ignores.

For our Vortex is uncompromising.

We must have the Past and the Future, Life simple, that is, to discharge ourselves in, and keep us pure for non-life, that is Art.

The Past and Future are the prostitutes Nature has provided.

Art is periodic escapes from this Brothel.

Artists put as much vitality and delight into this saintliness, and escape out, as most men do their escapes into similar places from respectable existence.

The Vorticist is at his maximum point of energy when stillest.

The Vorticist is not the Slave of Commotion, but it's Master.

The Vorticist does not suck up to Life.

He lets Life know its place in a Vorticist Universe !

III.

In a Vorticist Universe we don't get excited at what we have invented.

If we did it would look as though it had been a fluke.

.It is not a fluke.

10   We have no Verbotens.

There is one Truth, ourselves, and everything is permitted.

11   But we are not Templars.

We are proud, handsome and predatory.

We hunt machines, they are our favourite game.

We invent them and then hunt them down.

This is a great Vorticist age, a great still age of artists.

IV.

As to the lean belated Impressionism at present attempting to eke out a little life in these islands :

Our Vortex is fed up with your dispersals, reasonable chicken-men.

Our Vortex is proud of its polished sides.

Our Vortex will not hear of anything but its disastrous polished dance.

Our Vortex desires the immobile rythm of its swiftness.

Our Vortex rushes out like an angry dog at your Impressionistic fuss.

Our Vortex is white and abstract with its red-hot swiftness.

1 The Futurist Movement had been launched in 1909 by the Italian writer Filippo Tommaso Marinetti (1876-1944), who visited London in 1912. It made use of many gimmicks to promote interest.

2 George V had come to the throne in 1910.

3 David Lloyd George (1863-1945) was the leading Radical politician of the period.

4 The hostess wife of Alfred Mond (1868-1930), a well-known industrialist and Liberal politician, who had become a baronet in 1910.

5 The Sistine Chapel, decorated by Michelangelo.

6 Chephren or Khafre, a Pharoah of the IVth Dynasty, who built one of the Giza group of pyramids and whose head is believed to be represented on the nearby giant Sphinx.

7 The Futurists were enthusiastic about the beauty of machinery.

8 Oscar Wilde (1854-1960) had welcomed labour-saving machinery in his essay 'The Soul of Man under Socialism' (1891).

9 George Gissing (1857-1903) was mainly known for his novels of lower-class London Life, including *Demos* (1880) and *The Nether World* (1889).

10 Literally 'forbiddens'.

11 Knights Templar were charged in the Middle Ages with protecting pilgrims to the Holy Land; here, a chivalrous protector.

T.E. Hulme

Thomas Ernest Hulme (1883-1917) was an independent and pugnacious thinker and controversialist, interested in the Intuitionist philosophy of Henri Bergson (on whom he wrote in The New Age *in 1911). He organised a poetry club to which Flint and Pound belonged, meeting at the Eiffel Tower restaurant in Soho, at which he read the few Imagist poems published as the 'Complete Poetical Works of T.E. Hulme' in* The New Age *in January 1912, and as an Appendix in Pound's* Ripostes *(1912). He was killed in the Great War, leaving many projects uncompleted.*

7 From 'Romanticism and Classicism', c. 1914

Hulme's works were published in 1924 by Herbert Read as Speculations. *Essays on Humanism and the Philosophy of Art. The essay (of which pp.113, 117-20, 126-8, 132-3 are quoted) shows Hulme's thorough-going rejection of the whole tradition of romantic individualism.*

I want to maintain that after a hundred years of romanticism, we are in for a classical revival, and that the particular weapon of this new classical spirit, when it works in verse, will be fancy. And in this I imply the superiority of fancy–not superior generally or absolutely, for that would be obvious nonsense, but superior in the sense that we use the word in empirical ethics–good for something, superior for something. I shall have to prove then two things, first that a classical revival is coming, and, secondly, for its particular purposes, fancy will be superior to imagination.[1]

[...]

Put shortly, these are the two views, then. One, that man is intrinsically good, spoilt by circumstance; and the other that he is intrinsically limited, but disciplined by order and tradition to something fairly decent. To the one party man's nature is like a well, to the other like a bucket. The view which regards man as a well, a reservoir full of possibilities, I call the romantic; the one which regards

47

him as a very finite and fixed creature, I call the classical.

One may note here that the Church has always taken the classical view since the defeat of the Pelagian heresy[2] and the adoption of the sane classical dogma of original sin.

It would be a mistake to identify the classical view with that of materialism. On the contrary it is absolutely identical with the normal religious attitude. I should put it in this way: That part of the fixed nature of man is the belief in the Deity. This should be as fixed and true for every man as belief in the existence of matter and in the objective world. It is parallel to appetite, the instinct of sex, and all the other fixed qualities. Now at certain times, by the use of either force or rhetoric, these instincts have been suppressed—in Florence under Savonarola,[3] in Geneva under Calvin,[4] and here under the Roundheads. The inevitable result of such a process is that the repressed instinct bursts out in some abnormal direction. So with religion. By the perverted rhetoric of Rationalism, your natural instincts are suppressed and you are converted into an agnostic. Just as in the case of the other instincts, Nature has her revenge. The instincts that find their right and proper outlet in religion must come out in some other way. You don't believe in a God, so you begin to believe that man is a god. You don't believe in Heaven, so you begin to believe in a heaven on earth. In other words, you get romanticism. The concepts that are right and proper in their own sphere are spread over, and so mess up, falsify and blur the clear outlines of human experience. It is like pouring a pot of treacle over the dinner table. Romanticism then, and this is the best definition I can give of it, is spilt religion.

I must now shirk the difficulty of saying exactly what I mean by romantic and classical in verse. I can only say that it means the result of these two attitudes towards the cosmos, towards man, in so far as it gets reflected in verse. The romantic, because he thinks man infinite, must always be talking about infinite; and as there is always the bitter contrast between what you think you ought to be able to do and what man actually can, it always tends, in its later stages at any rate, to be gloomy. I really can't go any further than to say it is the reflection of these two temperaments, and point out examples of the different spirits. On the one hand I would take such diverse people as Horace,[5] most of the Elizabethans and the writers of the Augustan age, and on the other side Lamartine,[6] Hugo,[7] parts of Keats, Coleridge, Byron, Shelley and Swinburne.

I know quite well that when people think of classical and romantic in verse, the contrast at once comes into their mind between, say,

Racine[8] and Shakespeare. I don't mean this; the dividing line that I intend is here misplaced a little from the true middle. That Racine is on the extreme classical side I agree, but if you call Shakespeare romantic, you are using a different definition to the one I give. You are thinking of the difference between classic and romantic as being merely one between restraint and exuberance. I should say with Nietzsche that there are two kinds of classicism, the static and the dynamic.[9] Shakespeare is the classic of motion.

What I mean by classical in verse, then, is this. That even in the most imaginative flights there is always a holding back, a reservation. The classical poet never forgets this finiteness, this limit of man. He remembers always that he is mixed up with earth. He may jump, but he always returns back; he never flies away into the circumambient gas.

You might say if you wished that the whole of the romantic attitude seems to crystallise in verse round metaphors of flight. Hugo is always flying, flying over abysses, flying up into the eternal gases. The word infinite in every other line.

In the classical attitude you never seem to swing right along to the infinite nothing. If you say an extravagant thing which does exceed the limits inside which you know man to be fastened, yet there is always conveyed in some way at the end an impression of yourself standing outside it, and not quite believing it, or consciously putting it forward as a flourish. You never go blindly into an atmosphere more than the truth, an atmosphere too rarefied for man to breathe for long. You are always faithful to the conception of a limit. It is a question of pitch; in romantic verse you move at a certain pitch of rhetoric which you know, man being what he is, to be a little high-falutin. The kind of thing you get in Hugo or Swinburne. In the coming classical reaction that will feel just wrong.

[...]

I object even to the best of the romantics. I object still more to the receptive attitude. I object to the sloppiness which doesn't consider that a poem is a poem unless it is moaning or whining about something or other. I always think in this connection of the last line of a poem of John Webster's which ends with a request I cordially endorse:

End your moan and come away.[10]

The thing has got so bad now that a poem which is all dry and hard, a properly classical poem, would not be considered poetry at all. How many people now can lay their hands on their hearts and say they like either Horace or Pope? They feel a kind of chill when they read them.

The dry hardness which you get in the classics is absolutely repugnant to them. Poetry that isn't damp isn't poetry at all. They cannot see that accurate description is a legitimate object of verse. Verse to them always means a bringing in of some of the emotions that are grouped round the word infinite.

The essence of poetry to most people is that it must lead them to a beyond of some kind. Verse strictly confined to the earthly and the definite (Keats is full of it) might seem to them to be excellent writing, excellent craftsmanship, but not poetry. So much has romanticism debauched us, that, without some form of vagueness, we deny the highest.

In the classic it is always the light of ordinary day, never the light that never was on land or sea. It is always perfectly human and never exaggerated: man is always man and never a god.

But the awful result of romanticism is that, accustomed to this strange light, you can never live without it. Its effect on you is that of a drug.

There is a general tendency to think that verse means little else than the expression of unsatisfied emotion. People say: 'But how can you have verse without sentiment?' You see what it is: the prospect alarms them. A classical revival to them would mean the prospect of an arid desert and the death of poetry as they understand it, and could only come to fill the gap caused by that death. Exactly why this dry classical spirit should have a positive and legitimate necessity to express itself in poetry is utterly inconceivable to them. What this positive need is, I shall show later. It follows from the fact that there is another quality, not the emotion produced, which is at the root of excellence in verse. Before I get to this I am concerned with a negative thing, a theoretical point, a prejudice that stands in the way and is really at the bottom of this reluctance to understand classical verse.

It is an objection which ultimately I believe comes from a bad metaphysic of art. You are unable to admit the existence of beauty without the infinite being in some way or another dragged in.

The great aim is accurate, precise and definite description. The first thing is to recognise how extraordinarily difficult this is. It is no mere matter of carefulness; you have to use language, and language is by its very nature a communal thing; that is, it expresses never the exact thing but a compromise–that which is common to you, me and everybody. But each man sees a little differently, and to get out clearly and exactly what he does see, he must have a terrific struggle with language, whether it be with words or the technique of other arts. Language has its own special nature, its own conventions and communal ideas. It is only by a concentrated effort of the mind that you can hold it fixed to your own purpose. I always think that the fundamental process at the back of all the arts might be represented by the following metaphor. You know what I call architect's curves–flat pieces of wood with all different kinds of curvature. By a suitable selection from these you can draw approximately any curve you like. The artist I take to be the man who simply can't bear the idea of that 'approximately.' He will get the exact curve of what he sees whether it be an object or an idea in the mind. I shall here have to change my metaphor a little to get the process in his mind. Suppose that instead of your curved pieces of wood you have a springy piece of steel of the same types of curvature as the wood. Now the state of tension or concentration of mind, if he is doing anything really good in this struggle against the ingrained habit of the technique, may be represented by a man employing all his fingers to bend the steel out of its own curve and into the exact curve which you want. Something different to what it would assume naturally.

There are then two things to distinguish, first the particular faculty of mind to see things as they really are, and apart from the conventional ways in which you have been trained to see them. This is itself rare enough in all consciousness. Second, the concentrated state of mind, the grip over oneself which is necessary in the actual expression of what one sees. To prevent one falling into the conventional curves of ingrained technique, to hold on through infinite detail and trouble to the exact curve you want. Wherever you get this sincerity, you get the fundamental quality of good art without dragging in infinite or serious.

I can now get at that positive fundamental quality of verse which constitutes excellence, which has nothing to do with infinity, with mystery or with emotions.

1 Much Romantic thinking is based upon belief in the superiority of Imagination to Fancy, as explained by Coleridge in *Biographia Literaria* (1817), Chapter XIII.
2 Pelagius was a fourth/fifth-century British monk who denied the doctrine of original sin, by which every human being is innately sinful.
3 Fra Girolamo Savonarola (1452-98) was a puritanical Dominican monk, who led the popular party in Florence against the Medicis but was eventually executed as a heretic.
4 Jean Calvin (1504-64) was one of the leaders of the Reformation, and theocratic ruler of Geneva.
5 Quintus Horatius Flaccu (65-8 BC), the Roman poet.
6 Alphonse de Lamartine (1790-1869), French Romantic poet.
7 Victor Hugo (1802-85), French Romantic poet and dramatist.
8 Jean Racine (1639-99), French Classical dramatist.

9   Friedrich Nietzsche (1844-1900), the German philosopher, was a major influence on Hulme's group; the reference is to *The Birth of Tragedy* (1872).

10 From the scene leading to the Duchess's murder in *The Duchess of Malfi*, IV, ii; the usual reading is 'groan', not 'moan'.

Amy Lowell

Amy Lowell (1874-1925) was a wealthy American who came to London in 1914, and played a very active part in its literary life, especially in promoting Imagism. She contributed to the anthology Des Imagistes *(1914), and organised* Some Imagist Poets *in 1915, 1916 and 1917. Pound regarded these later anthologies as too inclusive and lacking in vigour. As he wrote to her in a letter on 1 August 1914, 'I should like the name "Imagisme" to retain some of its meaning. It stands, or I should like it to stand for hard light, clear edges. I can not trust any democratized committee to maintain that standard. Some will be splay-foot and some sentimental.' (D. D. Paige,* The Letters of Ezra Pound: 1907-41 *(New York, 1950), p. 38).*

Although she subsidised the publication, it is not clear whether the anonymous Preface was written by her. Richard Aldington (1892-1962) and H. D. (Hilda Doolittle (1886-1961)) were also much involved; see P. Jones, ed., Imagist Poetry *(1972), pp. 23-4.*

8 *Preface to* Some Imagist Poets, *1915*
The volume included contributions from Richard Aldington, H. D., and D.H. Lawrence.

In March, 1914, a volume appeared entitled *Des Imagistes*. It was a collection of the work of various young poets, presented together as a school. This school has been widely discussed by those interested in new movements in the arts, and has already become a household word. Differences of taste and judgment, however, have arisen among the contributors to that book; growing tendencies are forcing them along different paths. Those of us whose work appears in this volume have therefore decided to publish our collection under a new title, and we have been joined by two or three poets who did not contribute to the first volume, our wider scope making this possible.

In this new book we have followed a slightly different arrangement to that of the former Anthology. Instead of an arbitrary selction by an editor, each poet has been permitted to represent himself by the work he considers his best, the only stipulation being that it should not yet have appeared in book form. A sort of informal committee–consisting of more than half the authors here represented–have arranged the book and decided what should be printed and what omitted, but, as a general rule, the poets have been allowed absolute freedom in this direction, limitations of space only being imposed upon them. Also, to avoid any appearance of precedence, they have been put in alphabetical order.

As it has been suggested that much of the misunderstanding of the former volume was due to the fact we did not explain ourselves in a preface, we have thought it wise to tell the public what our aims are, and why we are banded together between one set of covers.

The poets in this volume do not represent a clique. Several of them are personally unknown to the others, but they are united by certain common principles, arrived at independently. These principles are not new; they have fallen into desuetude. They are the essentials of all great poetry, indeed of all great literature, and they are simply these:

1. To use the language of common speech, but to employ always the *exact* word, not the nearly-exact, nor the merely decorative word.

2. To create new rhythms–as the expression of new moods–and not to copy old rhythms, which merely echo old moods. We do not insist upon 'free-verse' as the only method of writing poetry. We fight for it as for a principle of liberty. We believe that the individuality of a poet may often be better expressed in free-verse than in conventional forms. In poetry, a new cadence means a new idea.

3. To allow absolute freedom in the choice of subject. It is not good art to write badly about aeroplanes and automobiles; nor is it necessarily bad art to write well about the past. We believe passionately in the artistic value of modern life, but we wish to point out that there is nothing so uninspiring nor so old-fashioned as an aeroplane of the year 1911.

4. To present an image (hence the name: 'Imagist'). We are not a school of painters, but we believe that poetry should render particulars exactly and not deal in vague generalities, however magnificent and sonorous. It is for this reason that we oppose the cosmic poet, who seems to us to shirk the real difficulties of his art.

5. To produce poetry that is hard and clear, never blurred nor indefinite.

6. Finally, most of us believe that concentration is of the very essence of poetry.

The subject of free-verse is too complicated to be discussed here. We may say briefly, that we attach the term to all that increasing amount of writing whose cadence is more marked, more definite, and closer knit than that of prose, but which is not so violently nor so obviously accented as the so-called 'regular verse.' We refer those interested in the question to the Greek Melic[1] poets, and to the many excellent French studies on the subject by such distinguished and well-equipped authors as Remy de Gourmont, Gustave Kahn, Georges Duhamel, Charles Vildrac, Henri Ghéon, Robert de Souza, André Spire, etc.

We wish it to be clearly understood that we do not represent an exclusive artistic sect; we publish our work together because of mutual artistic sympathy, and we propose to bring out our cooperative volume each year for a short term of years, until we have made a place for ourselves and our principles such as we desire.

1   Writers of poetry intended to be sung, especially the strophic odes. Aldington and H.D. had published a volume of classical translations entitled *Images, Old and new* in 1915.

James Joyce

Joyce (1882-1941) had left Ireland in 1902, to spend his later life in Trieste, Zurich and Paris. His volume of poetry Chamber Music *(1907) was followed by the short stories of* Dubliners *(1914):* A Portrait of the Artist as a Young Man *was serialized in* The Egoist *(1914-15);* Ulysses *was published in Paris in 1922, to become the most famous of Modernist fictions. Subsequently, Joyce worked on another long work, finally completed as* Finnegans Wake *in 1939.*

9 *From* A Portrait of the Artist as a Young Man, *1916*
In these extracts from the fifth section of the book, the young Stephen Dedalus is explaining his views on art to another student, Lynch.

Stephen went on:
–Pity is the feeling which arrests the mind in the presence of whatsoever is grave and constant in human sufferings and unites it with the human sufferer. Terror is the feeling which arrests the mind in the presence of whatsoever is grave and constant in human sufferings and unites it with the secret cause.
–Repeat, said Lynch.
Stephen repeated the definitions slowly.
–A girl got into a hansom a few days ago, he went on, in London. She was on her way to meet her mother whom she had not seen for many years. At the corner of a street the shaft of a lorry shivered the window of the hansom in the shape of a star. A long fine needle of the shivered glass pierced her heart. She died on the instant. The reporter called it a tragic death. It is not. It is remote from terror and pity according to the terms of my definitions.
–The tragic emotion, in fact, is a face looking two ways, towards terror and towards pity, both of which are phases of it. You see I use the word *arrest*. I mean that the tragic emotion is static. Or rather the dramatic emotion is. The feelings excited by improper art are kinetic, desire or loathing. Desire urges us to possess, to go to something;

loathing urges us to abandon, to go from something. The arts which excite them, pornographical or didactic, are therefore improper arts. The esthetic emotion (I used the general term) is therefore static. The mind is arrested and raised above desire and loathing.

–You say that art must not excite desire, said Lynch. I told you that one day I wrote my name in pencil on the backside of the Venus of Praxiteles in the Museum. Was that not desire?

–I speak of normal natures, said Stephen. You also told me that when you were a boy in that charming carmelite school you ate pieces of dried cowdung.

Lynch broke again into a whinny of laughter and again rubbed both his hands over his groins but without taking them from his pockets.

–O, I did! I did! he cried.

[...]

Even in literature, the highest and most spiritual art, the forms are often confused. The lyrical form is in fact the simplest verbal vesture of an instant of emotion, a rhythmical cry such as ages ago cheered on the man who pulled at the oar or dragged stones up a slope. He who utters it is more conscious of the instant of emotion than of himself as feeling emotion. The simplest epical form is seen emerging out of lyrical literature when the artist prolongs and broods upon himself as the centre of an epical event and this form progresses till the centre of emotional gravity is equidistant from the artist himself and from others. The narrative is no longer purely personal. The personality of the artist passes into the narration itself, flowing round and round the persons and the action like a vital sea. This progress you will see easily in that old English ballad *Turpin Hero* which begins in the first person and ends in the third person. The dramatic form is reached when the vitality which has flowed and eddied round each person fills every person with such vital force that he or she assumes a proper and intangible esthetic life. The personality of the artist, at first a cry or a cadence or a mood and then a fluid and lambent narrative, finally refines itself out of existence, impersonalizes itself, so to speak. The esthetic image in the dramatic form is life purified in and reprojected from the human imagination. The mystery of esthetic, like that of material creation, is accomplished. The artist, like the God of creation, remains within or behind or beyond or above his handiwork, invisible, refined out of existence, indifferent, paring his fingernails.

–Trying to refine them also out of existence, said Lynch.

A fine rain began to fall from the high veiled sky and they turned into the duke's lawn to reach the national library before the shower came.

–What do you mean, Lynch asked surlily, by prating about beauty and the imagination in this miserable Godforsaken island? No wonder the artist retired within or behind his handiwork after having perpetrated this country.

Ezra Pound

Pound (1885-1972) came to Europe in 1908, settling in London the following year, where his volumes of poetry were Personae *(1909),* Canzoni *(1911),* Ripostes *(1912),* Cathay *(1916),* Homage to Sextus Propertius *(1917) and* Hugh Selwyn Mauberley *(1920). He was active in promoting new approaches in all the arts through his critical journalism, being particularly involved with Imagism and Vorticism. Critical books were* The Spirit of Romance *(1910),* Pavannes and Divisions *(New York, 1918) and* Instigations *(New York, 1920).*

T.S. Eliot edited Literary Essays of Ezra Pound *in 1954. A wider coverage of his prose writings is* Selected Prose 1909-65, *ed. William Cookson (1973).*

10 'A Retrospect', 1918

This first appeared in Pavannes and Divisions, *but incorporated the earlier pieces 'A Few Don'ts for Imagistes' from* Poetry (Chicago), *I, 6 (March 1913), 200-6, and 'Prolegomena' from* Poetry Review *I, 2 (February 1912), 72-6.*

There has been so much scribbling about new fashion in poetry, that I may perhaps be pardoned this brief recapitulation and retrospect.

In the spring or early summer of 1912, 'H.D.',[1] Richard Aldington[2] and myself decided that we were agreed upon the three principles following:

1. Direct treatment of the 'thing' whether subjective or objective.
2. To use absolutely no word that does not contribute to the presentation.
3. As regarding rhythm: to compose in the sequence of the musical phrase, not in sequence of a metronome.

Upon many points of taste and of predilection we differed, but agreeing upon these three positions we thought we had as much right to a group name, at least as much right , as a number of French 'schools' proclaimed by Mr Flint in the August number of Harold Monro's magazine[3] for 1911.

This school has since been 'joined' or 'followed ' by numerous people who, whatever their merits, do not show any signs of agreeing with the second specification. Indeed *vers libre* has become as prolix and as verbose as any of the flaccid varieties that preceded it. It has brought faults of its own. The actual language and phrasing is often as bad as that of our elders without even the excuse that the words are shovelled in to fill a metric pattern or to complete the noise of rhythm-sound. Whether or no the phrases followed by the followers are musical must be left to the reader's decision. At times I can find a marked metre in 'vers libres', as stale and hackneyed as any pseudo-Swinburnian, at times the writers seem to follow no musical stucture whatever. But it is, on the whole, good that the field should be ploughed. Perhaps a few good poems have come from the new method, and if so it is justified.

Criticism is not a circumscription or a set of prohibitions. It provides fixed points of departure. It may startle a dull reader into alertness. That little of it which is good is mostly in stray phrases; or if it be an older artist helping a younger it is in great measure but rules of thumb, cautions gained by experience.

I set together a few phrases on practical working about the time the first remarks on imagisme were published. The first use of the word 'Imagiste' was in my note to T. E. Hulme's five poems, printed at the end of my 'Ripostes' in the autumn of 1912. I reprint my cautions from *Poetry* for March, 1913.

A FEW DON'TS

An 'Image' is that which presents an intellectual and emotional complex in an instant of time. I use the term 'complex' rather in the technical sense employed by the newer psychologists, such as Hart, though we might not agree absolutely in our application.

It is the presentation of such a 'complex' instantaneously which gives that sense of sudden liberation; that sense of freedom from time limits and space limits; that sense of sudden growth, which we experience in the presence of the greatest works of art.

It is better to present one Image in a lifetime than to produce voluminous works.

All this, however, some may consider open to debate. The immediate necessity is to tabulate A LIST OF DON'TS for those beginning to write verses. I can not put all of them into Mosaic negative.

To begin with, consider the three propositions (demanding direct treatment, economy of words, and the sequence of the musical phrase), not as dogma – never consider anything as dogma – but as the result of long contemplation, which, even if it is some one else's contemplation, may be worth consideration.

Pay no attention to the criticism of men who have never themselves written a notable work. Consider the discrepancies between the actual writing of the Greek poets and dramatists, and the theories of the Graeco-Roman grammarians, concocted to explain their metres.

LANGUAGE

Use no superfluous word, no adjective which does not reveal something.

Don't use such an expression as 'dim lands of *peace*'. It dulls the image. It mixes an abstraction with the concrete. It comes from the writer's not realizing that the natural object is always the *adequate* symbol.

Go in fear of abstractions. Do not retell in mediocre verse what has already been done in good prose. Don't think any intelligent person is going to be deceived when you try to shirk all the difficulties of the unspeakably difficult art of good prose by chopping your composition into line lengths.

What the expert is tired of today the public will be tired of tomorrow.

Don't imagine that the art of poetry is any simpler than the art of music, or that you can please the expert before you have spent at least as much effort on the art of verse as the average piano teacher spends on the art of music.

Be influenced by as many great artists as you can, but have the decency either to acknowledge the debt outright, or to try to conceal it.

Don't allow 'influence' to mean merely that you mop up the particular decorative vocabulary of some one or two poets whom you happen to admire. A Turkish war correspondent was recently caught red-handed babbling in his despatches of 'dove-grey' hills, or else it was 'pearl-pale', I can not remember.

Use either no ornament or good ornament.

RHYTHM AND RHYME

Let the candidate fill his mind with the finest cadences he can discover, preferably in a foreign language,[4] so that the meaning of the words may be less likely to divert his attention from the movement; e.g. Saxon charms, Hebridean Folk Songs, the verse of Dante, and the lyrics of Shakespeare—if he can dissociate the vocabulary from the cadence. Let him dissect the lyrics of Goethe coldly into their component sound values, syllables long and short, stressed and unstressed, into vowels and consonants.

It is not necessary that a poem should rely on its music, but if it does rely on its music that music must be such as will delight the expert.

Let the neophyte know assonance and alliteration, rhyme immediate and delayed, simple and polyphonic, as a musician would expect to know harmony and counterpoint and all the minutiae of his craft. No time is too great to give to these matters or to any one of them, even if the artist seldom have need of them.

Don't imagine that a thing will 'go' in verse just because it's too dull to go in prose.

Don't be 'viewy'–leave that to the writers of pretty little philosophic essays. Don't be descriptive; remember that the painter can describe a landscape much better than you can, and that he has to know a deal more about it.

When Shakespeare talks of the 'Dawn in russet mantle clad' he presents something which the painter does not present. There is in this line of his nothing that one can call description; he presents.

Consider the way of the scientists rather than the way of an advertising agent for a new soap.

The scientist does not expect to be acclaimed as a great scientist until he has *discovered* something. He begins by learning what has been discovered already. He goes from that point onward. He does not bank on being a charming fellow personally. He does not expect his friends to applaud the results of his freshman class work. Freshmen in poetry are unfortunately not confined to a definite and recognizable class room. They are 'all over the shop'. Is it any wonder 'the public is indifferent to poetry?'

Don't chop your stuff into separate *iambs*. Don't make each line stop dead at the end, and then begin every next line with a heave. Let the beginning of the next line catch the rise of the rhythm wave, unless you want a definite longish pause.

In short, behave as a musician, a good musician, when dealing with that phase of your art which has exact parallels in music. The same laws govern, and you are bound by no others.

Naturally, your rhythmic structure should not destroy the shape of your words, or their natural sound, or their meaning. It is improbable that, at the start, you will be able to get a rhythm-structure strong enough to affect them very much, though you may fall a victim to all sorts of false stopping due to line ends and caesurae.

The Musician can rely on pitch and the volume of the orchestra. You can not. The term harmony is misapplied in poetry; it refers to simultaneous sounds of different pitch. There is, however, in the best verse a sort of residue of sound which remains in the ear of the hearer and acts more or less as an organ-base.

A rhyme must have in it some slight element of surprise if it is to give pleasure; it need not be bizarre or curious, but it must be well used if used at all.

Vide further Vildrac and Duhamel's notes on rhyme in *Technique Poétique.*[5]

That part of your poetry which strikes upon the imaginative *eye* of the reader will lose nothing by translation into a foreign tongue; that which appeals to the ear can reach only those who take it in the original.

Consider the definiteness of Dante's presentation, as compared with Milton's rhetoric. Read as much of Wordsworth as does not seem too unutterably dull.

If you want the gist of the matter go to Sappho, Catullus, Villon, Heine when he is in the vein, Gautier when he is not too frigid; or, if you have not the tongues, seek out the leisurely Chaucer.[6] Good prose will do you no harm, and there is good discipline to be had by trying to write it.

Translation is likewise good training, if you find that your original matter 'wobbles' when you try to rewrite it. The meaning of the poem to be translated can not 'wobble'.

If you are using a symmetrical form, don't put in what you want to say and then fill up the remaining vacuums with slush.

Don't mess up the perception of one sense by trying to define it in terms of another. This is usually only the result of being too lazy to find the exact word. To this clause there are possibly exceptions.

The first three simple prescriptions will throw out nine-tenths of all the bad poetry now accepted as standard and classic; and will prevent you from many a crime of production.

' . . . *Mais d'abord il faut être un poète*', as MM. Duhamel and Vildrac have said at the end of their little book, *'Notes sur la Technique Poétique.'*

Since March 1913, Ford Madox Hueffer has pointed out that Wordsworth was so intent on the ordinary or plain word that he never thought of hunting for *le mot juste.*

John Butler Yeats has handled or man-handled Wordsworth and the Victorians, and his criticism, contained in letters to his son, is now printed and available.[7]

I do not like writing *about* art, my first, at least I think it was my first essay on the subject, was a protest against it.

PROLEGOMENA

Time was when the poet lay in a green field with his head against a tree and played his diversion on a ha'penny whistle, and Caesar's predecessors conquered the earth, and the predecessors of golden Crassus[8] embezzled, and fashions had their say, and let him alone. And presumably he was fairly content in this circumstance, for I have small doubt that the occasional passerby, being attracted by curiosity to know why any one should lie under a tree and blow diversion on a ha'penny whistle, came and conversed with him, and that among these passers-by there was on occasion a person of charm or a young lady who had not read *Man and Superman*,[9] and looking back upon this naïve state of affairs we call it the age of gold.

Metastasio,[10] and he should know if any one, assures us that this age endures—even though the modern poet is expected to holloa his verses down a speaking tube to the editors of cheap magazines—S. S. McClure,[11] or some one of that sort—even though hordes of authors meet in dreariness and drink healths to the 'Copyright Bill'; even though these things be, the age of gold pertains. Imperceivably, if you like, but pertains. You meet unkempt Amyclas[12] in a Soho restaurant and chant together of dead and forgotten things—it is a manner of speech among poets to chant of dead, half-forgotten things, there seems no special harm in it; it has always been done—and it's rather better to be a clerk in the Post Office than to look after a lot of stinking, verminous sheep—and at another hour of the day one substitutes the drawing-room for the restaurant and tea is probably more palatable than mead and mare's milk, and little cakes than honey. And in this fashion one survives the resignation of Mr Balfour,[13] and the iniquities of the American customs-house, *e quel bufera infernal*,[14] the periodical press. And then in the middle of it, there being apparently no other person at once capable and available one is stopped and asked to explain oneself.

I begin on the chord thus querulous, for I would much rather lie on what is left of Catullus'[15] parlour floor and speculate the azure beneath it and the hills off to Salo and Riva with their forgotten gods moving unhindered amongst them, than discuss any processes and theories of art whatsoever. I would rather play tennis. I shall not argue.

CREDO

Rhythm.—I believe in an 'absolute rhythm', a rhythm, that is, in poetry which corresponds exactly to the emotion or shade of emotion to be expressed. A man's rhythm must be interpretative, it will be, therefore, in the end, his own, uncounterfeiting, uncounterfeitable.

Symbols. – I believe that the proper and perfect symbol is the natural object, that if a man use 'symbols' he must so use them that their symbolic function does not obtrude; so that *a* sense, and the poetic quality of the passage, is not lost to those who do not understand the symbol as such, to whom, for instance, a hawk is a hawk.

Technique. – I believe in technique as the test of man's sincerity; in law when it is ascertainable; in the trampling down of every convention that impedes or obscures the determination of the law, or the precise rendering of the impulse.

Form. – I think there is a 'fluid' as well as a 'solid' content, that some poems may have form as a tree has form, some as water poured into a vase. That most symmetrical forms have certain uses. That a vast number of subjects cannot be precisely, and therefore not properly rendered in symmetrical forms.

'Thinking that alone worthy wherein the whole art is employed'.[16] I think the artist should master all known forms and systems of metric, and I have with some persistence set about doing this, searching particularly into those periods wherein the systems came to birth or attained their maturity. It has been complained, with some justice, that I dump my note-book on the public. I think that only after a long struggle will poetry attain such a degree of development, or, if you will, modernity, that it will vitally concern people who are accustomed, in prose, to Henry James and Anatole France,[17] in music to Debussy.[18] I am constantly contending that it took two centuries of Provence and one of Tuscany to develop the media of Dante's masterwork, that it took the latinists of the Renaissance, and the Pleiade,[19] and his own age of painted speech to prepare Shakespeare his tools. It is tremendously important that great poetry be written, it makes no jot of difference who writes it. The experimental demonstrations of one man may save the time of many – hence my furore over Arnaut Daniel[20] – if a man's experiments try out one new rime, or dispense conclusively with one iota of currently accepted nonsense, he is merely playing fair with his colleagues when he chalks up his result.

No man ever writes very much poetry that 'matters'. In bulk, that is, no one produces much that is final, and when a man is not doing this highest thing, this saying the thing once for all and perfectly; when he is not matching Ποικιλόθρον’, ἀθάνατ’ ’Αφρόδιτᾶ,[21] or 'Hist – said Kate the Queen',[22] he had much better be making the sorts of experiment which may be of use to him in his later work, or to his successors.

'The lyf so short, the craft so long to lerne.'[23] It is a foolish thing for a man to begin his work on a too narrow foundation, it is a disgraceful thing for a man's work not to show steady growth and increasing fineness from first to last.

As for 'adaptations'; one finds that all the old masters of painting recommend to their pupils that they begin by copying masterwork, and proceed to their own composition.

As for 'Every man his own poet', the more every man knows about poetry the better. I believe in every one writing poetry who wants to; most do. I believe in every man knowing enough of music to play 'God bless our home' on the harmonium, but I do not believe in every man giving concerts and printing his sin.

The mastery of any art is the work of a lifetime. I should not discriminate between the 'amateur' and the 'professional'. Or rather I should discriminate between the amateur and the expert. It is certain that the present chaos will endure until the Art of poetry has been preached down the amateur gullet, until there is such a general understanding of the fact that poetry is an art and not a pastime; such a knowledge of technique; of technique of surface and technique of content, that the amateurs will cease to try to drown out the masters.

If a certain thing was said once for all in Atlantis or Arcadia, in 450 Before Christ or in 1290 after, it is not for us moderns to go saying it over, or to go obscuring the memory of the dead by saying the same thing with less skill and less conviction.

My pawing over the ancients and semi-ancients has been one struggle to find out what has been done, once for all, better than it can ever be done again, and to find out what remains for us to do, and plenty does remain, for if we still feel the same emotions as those which launched the thousand ships, it is quite certain that we come on these feelings differently, through different nuances, by different intellectual gradations. Each age has its own abounding gifts yet only some ages transmute them into matter of duration. No good poetry is ever written in a manner twenty years old, for to write in such a manner shows conclusively that the writer thinks from books, convention and *cliché*, and not from life, yet a man feeling the divorce of life and his art may naturally try to resurrect a forgotten mode if he finds in that mode some leaven, or if he think he sees in it some element lacking in contemporary art which might unite that art again to its sustenance, life.

In the art of Daniel and Cavalcanti,[24] I have seen that precision which I miss in the Victorians, that explicit rendering, be it of external nature, or of emotion. Their testimony is of the eyewitness, their symptoms are first hand.

As for the nineteenth century, with all respect to its achievements, I think we shall look back upon it as a rather blurry, messy sort of a period, a rather sentimentalistic, mannerish sort of a period. I say this without any self-righteousness, with no self-satisfaction.

As for there being a 'movement' or my being of it, the conception of poetry as a 'pure art' in the sense in which I use the term, revived with Swinburne. From the puritanical revolt to Swinburne,[25] poetry had been merely the vehicle–yes, definitely, Arthur Symon's[26] scruples and feelings about the word not withholding–the ox-cart and post-chaise for transmitting thoughts poetic or otherwise. And perhaps the 'great Victorians', though it is doubtful, and assuredly the 'nineties' continued the development of the art, confining their improvements, however, chiefly to sound and to refinements of manner.

Mr Yeats has once and for all stripped English poetry of its perdamnable rhetoric. He has boiled away all that is not poetic–and a good deal that is. He has become a classic in his own lifetime and *nel mezzo del cammin.*[27] He has made our poetic idiom a thing pliable, a speech without inversions.

Robert Bridges,[28] Maurice Hewlett[29] and Frederic Manning[30] are in their different ways seriously concerned with overhauling the metric, in testing the language and its adaptability to certain modes. Ford Hueffer is making some sort of experiments in modernity.[31] The Provost of Oriel continues his translation of the *Divina Commedia.*[32]

As to Twentieth century poetry, and the poetry which I expect to see written during the next decade or so, it will, I think, move against poppy-cock, it will be harder and saner, it will be what Mr Hewlett calls 'nearer the bone'. It will be as much like granite as it can be, its force will lie in its truth, its interpretative power (of course, poetic force does always rest there); I mean it will not try to seem forcible by rhetorical din, and luxurious riot. We will have fewer painted adjectives impeding the shock and stroke of it. At least for myself, I want it so, austere, direct, free from emotional slither.

What is there now, in 1917, to be added?

RE VERS LIBRE

I think the desire for vers libre is due to the sense of quantity reasserting itself after years of starvation. But I doubt if we can take over, for English, the rules of quantity laid down for Greek and Latin, mostly by Latin grammarians.

I think one should write vers libre only when one 'must', that is to say, only when the 'thing' builds up a rhythm more beautiful than that of set metres, or more real, more a part of the emotion of the 'thing', more germane, intimate, interpretative than the measure of regular accentual verse; a rhythm which discontents one with set iambic or set anapaestic.

Eliot has said the thing very well when he said, 'No *vers* is *libre* for the man who wants to do a good job.'[33]

As a matter of detail, there is vers libre with accent heavily marked as a drum-beat (as par example my 'Dance Figure'),[34] and on the other hand I think I have gone as far as can profitably be gone in the other direction (and perhaps too far). I mean I do not think one can use to any advantage rhythms much more tenuous and imperceptible than some I have used. I think progress lies rather in an attempt to approximate classical quantitative metres (NOT to copy them) than in a carelessness regarding such things.

I agree with John Yeats on the relation of beauty to certitude. I prefer satire, which is due to emotion, to any sham of emotion.

I have had to write, or at least I have written a good deal about art, sculpture, painting and poetry. I have seen what seemed to me the best of contemporary work reviled and obstructed. Can any one write prose of permanent or durable interest when he is merely saying for one year what nearly every one will say at the end of three or four years? I have been battistrada[35] for a sculptor, a painter, a novelist, several poets. I wrote also of certain French writers in *The New Age* in nineteen twelve or eleven.[36]

I would much rather that people would look at Brzeska's sculpture and Lewis's drawings, and that they would read Joyce, Jules Romains,[37] Eliot, than that they should read what I have said of these men, or that I should be asked to republish argumentative essays and reviews.

All that the critic can do for the reader or audience or spectator is to focus his gaze or audition. Rightly or wrongly I think my blasts and essays have done their work, and that more people are now likely to go to the sources than are likely to read this book.

Jammes's[38] 'Existences' in *'La Triomphe de la Vie'* is available. So are his early poems. I think we need a convenient anthology rather than descriptive criticism. Carl Sandburg[39] wrote me from Chicago, 'It's hell when poets can't afford to buy each other's books.' Half the people who care, only borrow. In America so few people know each other that the difficulty lies more than half in distribution. Perhaps one should make an anthology: Romains's 'Un Etre en Marche' and 'Prières', Vildrac's 'Visite'. Retrospectively the fine wrought work of

Laforgue, the flashes of Rimbaud, the hard-bit lines of Tristan Corbière, Tailhade's sketches in 'Poèmes Aristophanesques', the 'Litanies' of De Gourmont.[40]

It is difficult at all times to write of the fine arts, it is almost impossible unless one can accompany one's prose with many reproductions. Still I would seize this chance or any chance to reaffirm my belief in Wyndham Lewis's genius, both in his drawings and his writings. And I would name an out of the way prose book, the *Scenes and Portraits* of Frederic Manning, as well as James Joyce's short stories and novel, 'Dubliners' and the now well known 'Portrait of the Artist' as well as Lewis' 'Tarr', if, that is, I may treat my strange reader as if he were a new friend come into the room, intent on ransacking my bookshelf.

ONLY EMOTION ENDURES

'Only emotion endures.' Surely it is better for me to name over the few beautiful poems that still ring in my head than for me to search my flat for back numbers of periodicals and rearrange all that I have said about friendly and hostile writers.

The first twelve lines of Padraic Colum's[41] 'Drover'; his 'O Woman shapely as a swan, on your account I shall not die'; Joyce's 'I hear an army'; the lines of Yeats that ring in my head and in the heads of all young men of my time who care for poetry: Braseal and the Fisherman, 'The fire that stirs about her when she stirs'; the later lines of 'The Scholars', the faces of the Magi; William Carlos Williams's[42] 'Postlude', Aldington's version of 'Atthis', and 'H.D.'s' waves like pine tops, and her verse in 'Des Imagistes' the first anthology; Hueffer's 'How red your lips are' in his translation from Von der Vogelweide, his 'Three Ten', the general effect of his 'On Heaven'; his sense of the prose values or prose qualities in poetry; his ability to write poems that half-chant and are spoiled by a musician's additions; beyond these a poem by Alice Corbin,[43] 'One City Only', and another ending 'But sliding water over a stone'. These things have worn smooth in my head and I am not through with them, nor with Aldington's 'In Via Sestina' nor his other poems in 'Des Imagistes', though people have told me their flaws.[44] It may be that their content is too much embedded in me for me to look back at the words.

I am almost a different person when I come to take up the argument for Eliot's poems.

1 Hilda Doolittle (1886-1961), novelist and poet, had come to Europe from America in 1911.
2 Richard Aldington (1892-1962), poet and critic, who married 'H.D.' in 1913.

3   *The Poetry Review*; the date was actually August 1912. See headnote to Flint entry, p.40 above.

4   Pound's note: 'This is for rhythm, his vocabulary must of course be found in his native tongue'.

5   Charles Vildrac (1882-1971) and Georges Duhamel (1884-1966) had jointly published *Notes sur la technique poétique* in 1911.

6   Poets respected by Pound for the definiteness of their visual observation.

7   Pound had edited *Passages from the Letters of John Butler Yeats* for the Cuala Press, Dublin, 1917.

8   Licinus Crassus, Roman consul of the 1st century BC, known for his avarice.

9   The play in 1903 by G. Bernard Shaw concerning the Life Force.

10 Pietro Trapassi, known as Metastasio (1698-1782), was an Italian Arcadian poet and opera-writer.

11 McClure (1857-1949) was a successful American editor and publisher, who had founded *McClure's Magazine* in 1893.

12 Evidently a pastoral poet, but not a historical figure.

13 A.J. Balfour (1848-1930) resigned the leadership of the Conservative Party in 1911.

14 'and that infernal absurdity'.

15 Gaius Valerius Catullus (*c.*84–*c.*54BC), Roman lyric poet.

16 Pound cites as his source Dante's *De Volgari Eloquio (De vulgari eloquentia)*, which discusses vernacular language in relation to poetry, and the technique of the *canzone*.

17 (1844-1924), French novelist.

18 Claude Debussy (1862-1918), the French composer.

19 A distinguished group of late sixteenth-century French poets including Pierre de Ronsard and Joachim du Bellay.

20 Daniel (*c.*1180–*c.*1210) was one of the finest Troubadour poets, particularly admired by Pound.

21 'Richly-enthroned, immortal Aphrodite'; the opening words of Sappho's 'Hymn to Aphrodite' of the 7th century BC.

22 From the Page's Song in Robert Browning's *Pippa Passes* (1841), Part II.

23 The opening line of Geoffrey Chaucer's *The Parlement of Foules* (*c.*1383), translated from the Greek aphorism of Hippocrates.

24 Guido Cavalcanti (*c.*1260-1300), early Italian poet.

25 Algernon Charles Swinburne (1837-1909), the Victorian poet, was admired by Pound for the musicality of his language and his disregard for Victorian morality.

26 Arthur Symons (1865-1945) was a poet and critic, whose *The Symbolist Movement in Literature* (1899) was dedicated to Yeats.

27 'In the middle of the way'–the opening words of Dante's *Inferno*, referring to middle age.

28 Bridges (1844-1930) was a scholarly poet, author of *Milton's Prosody* (1893) and a founder of the Society for Pure English.

29 Hewlett (1861-1923) was mainly known as a historical novelist, but also wrote criticism and poetry.

30 Manning (1887-1935) was an Australian writer who lived in London; his *Scenes and Portraits* had appeared in 1909.

31 Ford published *Songs from London* in 1910, and *Collected Poems* in 1913.

32 Dr Charles Shadwell (1840-1919), Provost of Oriel College, Oxford 1905-14, translated Dante's *Purgatorio* (1892) and *Paradiso* (1915), employing Marvellian stanzas.

33 Perhaps a summary of the argument of Eliot's 'Reflections on *Vers Libre*' in the *New Statesman*, 3 March 1917.

34 Pound's poem 'Dance Figure for the Marriage in Cana of Galilee' had appeared in his *Lustra* in 1916.

35 Italian: 'herald'.

36 Pound published seven articles with the title 'The Approach to Paris' in the *New Age* between 4th September and 16th October 1913.

37 Romains (1885-1972) was a French poet and novelist; he published *La Vie unanime* in 1908, *Un Etre en Marche* in 1910, and *Odes et Prières* in 1913.

38 Francis Jammes (1868-1938) was a French religious poet.

39 Carl Sandburg (1878-1967) was an American poet who employed free verse and colloquialism.

40 French poets admired by Pound: Jules Laforgue (1860-87), Arthur Rimbaud (1854-91), Tristan Corbière (1845-75), Laurent Tailhade (1854-1919) whose 'Poèmes Aristophaniques' appeared in 1904, and Rémy de Gourmont (1885-1915), whose 'Litanies de la Rose' appeared in *Divertissements* in 1912.

41 Colum (1881-1972) was an Irish poet.

42 Williams (1883-1963) practised as a doctor in Rutherford, and wrote much poetry, the *Poems* (1909) and *The Tempers* (1913) making use of Imagist techniques.

43 Alice Corbin Henderson (1881-1949) was an editor of *Poetry* (Chicago) from 1912 to 1916; she published *The Spinning Woman of the Sky* in 1912.

44 It will be noted that all the poems quoted are from writers associated with Pound and the Imagist movement, many of them included in the Imagist anthologies.

11 'Wyndham Lewis' 1920

Published in Instigations *(1920). Pound had previously published 'Wyndham Lewis' in* Egoist *I, 12 (15 June 1914), 233-4, and a review of* Tarr *in* Little Review *IV (11 March 1918), 35.*

The signal omission from my critical papers is an adequate book on Wyndham Lewis; my excuses, apart from limitations of time, must be that Mr Lewis is alive and quite able to speak for himself, secondly that one may print half-tone reproductions of sculpture, for however unsatisfactory they be, they pretend to be only half-tones, and could not show more than they do; but the reproduction of drawings and paintings invites all sorts of expensive process impracticable during the years of war. When the public or the 'publishers' are ready for a volume of Lewis, suitably illustrated, I am ready to write in the letterpress, though Mr Lewis would do it better than I could.

He will rank among the great instigators and great inventors of design; there is mastery in his use of various media (my own interest in his work centres largely in the 'drawing' completed with inks, water-colour, chalk, etc.). His name is constantly bracketed with Gaudier, Picasso, Joyce, but these are fortuitous couplings. Lewis' painting is further from the public than were the carvings of Gaudier;

Lewis is an older artist, maturer, fuller of greater variety and invention. His work is almost unknown to the public. His name is wholly familiar, BLAST is familiar, the 'Timon' portfolio[1] has been seen.

I had known him for several years, known him as an artist, but I had no idea of his scope until he began making his preparations to go into the army; so careless had he been of any public or private approval. The 'work' lay in piles on the floor of an attic; and from it we gathered most of the hundred or hundred and twenty drawings which now form the bases of the Quinn collection[2] and of the Baker collection (now in the South Kensington museum).[3]

As very few people have seen all of these of pictures very few people are in any position to contradict me. There are three of his works in this room and I can attest their wearing capacity; as I can attest the duration of my regret for the Red drawing now in the Quinn collection which hung here for some months waiting shipment; as I can attest the energy and vitality that filled this place while forty drawings of the Quinn assortment stood here waiting also; a demonstration of the difference between 'cubism', *nature-morte-ism* and the vortex of Lewis: sun, energy, sombre emotion, clean-drawing, disgust, penetrating analysis, from the qualities finding literary expression in *Tarr* to the stasis of the Red Duet,[4] from the metallic gleam of the 'Timon' portfolio to the velvet-suavity of the later 'Timon' of the Baker collection.

The animality and the animal satire, the dynamic and metallic properties, the social satire, on the one hand, the sunlight, the utter cleanness of the Red Duet, are all points in an astounding circumference, which will, until the work is adequately reproduced, have more or less to be taken on trust by the 'wider' public.

The novel *Tarr* is in print and no one need bother to read my critiques of it. It contains much that Joyce's work does not contain, but differentiations between the two authors are to the detriment of neither, one tries solely to discriminate qualities: hardness, fullness, abundance, weight, finish, all terms used sometimes with derogatory and sometimes with laudative intonation, or at any rate valued by one auditor and depreciated by another. The English prose fiction of my decade is the work of this pair of authors.

TARR, BY WYNDHAM LEWIS

Tarr is the most vigorous and volcanic English novel of our time. Lewis is the rarest of phenomena, an Englishman who has achieved the triumph of being also a European. He is the only English writer who can be compared with Dostoievsky, and he is more rapid than

Dostoiesky, his mind travels with greater celerity, with more unexpectedness, but he loses none of Dostoievsky's effect of mass and of weight.

Tarr is a man of genius surrounded by the heavy stupidities of the half-cultured latin quarter; the book delineates his explosions in this oleaginous milieu; as well as the débâcle of the unintelligent emotion-dominated Kreisler. They are the two titanic characters in contemporary English fiction. Wells's clerks, Bennett's 'cards' and even Conrad's Russian villains do not 'bulk up' against them.

Only in James Joyce's *Stephen Dedalus* does one find an equal intensity, and Joyce is, by comparison, cold and meticulous, where Lewis is, if uncouth, at any rate brimming with energy, the man with a leaping mind.

Despite its demonstrable faults I do not propose to attack this novel. It is a serious work, it is definitely an attempt to express, and very largely a success in expressing something. The 'average novel', the average successful commercial proposition at 6s. per 300 to 600 pages is nothing of the sort; it is merely a third-rate mind's imitation of a perfectly well-known type-novel; of let us say Dickens, or Balzac or Sir A. Conan-Doyle,[5] or Hardy, or Mr Wells, or Mrs Ward,[6] or some other and less laudable proto- or necro-type.

A certain commercial interest attaches to the sale of these mimicries and a certain purely technical or trade or clique interest may attach to the closeness of 'skill' in the aping, or to the 'application' of a formula. The 'work', the opus, has a purely narcotic value, it serves to soothe the tired mind of the reader, to take said 'mind' off its 'business' (whether that business be lofty, 'intellectual', humanitarian, sordid, acquisitive, or other). There is only one contemporary English work with which *Tarr* can be compared, namely James Joyce's utterly different *Portrait of the Artist*. The appearance of either of these novels would be a recognized literary event had it occurred in any other country in Europe.

Joyce's novel is a triumph of actual writing. The actual arrangement of the words is worth any author's study. Lewis on the contrary, is, in the actual writing, faulty. His expression is as bad as that of Meredith's[7] floppy sickliness. In place of Meredith's mincing we have something active and 'disagreeable'. But we have at any rate the percussions of a highly energized mind.

In both Joyce and Lewis we have the insistent utterance of men who are once for all through with the particular inanities of Shavian-Bennett, and with the particular oleosities of the Wellsian genre.

The faults of Mr Lewis' writing can be examined in the first twenty-five pages. Kreisler is the creation of the book. He is roundly and objectively set before us. Tarr is less clearly detached from his creator. The author has evidently suspected this, for he has felt the need of disclaiming Tarr in a preface.

Tarr, like his author, is a man with an energized mind. When Tarr talks at length; when Tarr gets things off his chest, we suspect that the author also is getting them off his own chest. Herein the technique is defective. It is also defective in that it proceeds by general descriptive statements in many cases where the objective presentment of single and definite acts would be more effective, more convincing.

It differs from the general descriptiveness of cheap fiction in that these general statements are often a very profound reach for the expression of verity. In brief, the author is trying to get the truth and not merely playing baby-battledore among phrases. When Tarr talks little essays and makes aphorisms they are often of intrinsic interest, are even unforgettable. Likewise, when the author comments upon Tarr, he has the gift of phrase, vivid, biting, pregnant, full of suggestion.

The engaging if unpleasant character, Tarr, is placed in an unpleasant milieu, a milieu very vividly 'done'. The reader retains no doubts concerning the verity and existence of this milieu (Paris or London is no matter, though the scene is, nominally, in Paris). It is the existence where:

'Art is the smell of oil paint, Henri Murger's *Vie de Bohème*,[8] corduroy trousers, the operatic Italian model...quarter given up to Art–Letters and other things are round the corner.

'...permanent tableaux of the place, disheartening as a Tussaud's of The Flood.'

Tarr's first impact is with 'Hobson', whose 'dastardly face attempted to portray delicacies of common sense, and gossamer-like back-slidings into the Inane, that would have puzzled a bile-specialist. He would occasionally exploit his blackguardly appearance and blacksmith's muscles for a short time...his strong piercing laugh threw A.B.C.[9] waitresses into confusion'.

This person wonders if Tarr is a 'sound bird'. Tarr is not a sound bird. His conversational attack on Hobson proceeds by a brandishing of false dilemma, but neither Hobson nor his clan, nor indeed any of the critics of the novel (to date) have observed that this is Tarr's faulty weapon. Tarr's contempt for Hobson is as adequate as it is justifiable.

'Hobson, he considered, was a crowd.–You could not say he was an individual.–He was a set. He sat there a cultivated audience.–He had the aplomb and absence of self-consciousness of numbers, of the herd – of those who know they are not alone.…

'For distinguishing feature Hobson possessed a distinguished absence of personality.… Hobson was an humble investor.'

Tarr addresses him with some frankness on the subject:

'As an off-set for your prying, scurvy way of peeping into my affairs you must offer your own guts, such as they are.…

'You have joined yourself to those who hush their voices to hear what other people are saying.…

'Your plumes are not meant to fly with, but merely to slouch and skip along the surface of the earth. – You wear the livery of a ridiculous set, you are a cunning and sleek domestic. No thought can come out of your head before it has slipped on its uniform. All your instincts are drugged with a malicious languor, an arm, a respectability, invented by a set of old women and mean, cadaverous little boys.'

Hobson opened his mouth, had a movement of the body to speak. But he relapsed.

'You reply, "What is all this fuss about? I have done the best for myself." – I am not suited for any heroic station, like yours. I live sensibly, cultivating my vegetable ideas, and also my roses and Victorian lilies. – I do no harm to anybody.'

'That is not quite the case. That is a little inexact. Your proceedings possess a herdesque astuteness; in the scale against the individual weighing less than the Yellow Press, yet being a closer and meaner attack. Also you are essentially *spies*, in a scurvy, safe and well-paid service, as I told you before. You are disguised to look like the thing it is your function to betray – What is your position? – You have bought for eight hundred pounds at an aristocratic educational establishment a complete mental outfit, a programme of manners. For four years you trained with other recruits. You are now a perfectly disciplined social unit, with a profound *esprit de corps*. The Cambridge set that you represent is an average specimen, a cross between a Quaker, a Pederast, and a Chelsea artist – Your Oxford brothers, dating from the Wilde decade, are a stronger body. The Chelsea artists are much less flimsy. The Quakers are powerful rascals. You represent, my Hobson, the *dregs* of Anglo-Saxon civilization! There is nothing softer on earth. – Your flabby potion is a mixture of the lees of Liberalism, the poor froth blown off the decadent nineties, the wardrobe-leavings of a vulgar Bohemianism with its headquarters in Chelsea!

'You are concentrated, systematic slop. – There is nothing in the universe to be said for you.…

'A breed of mild pervasive cabbages, has set up a wide and creeping

rot in the West of Europe.—They make it indirectly a peril and a tribulation for live things to remain in the neighbourhood. You are a systematizing and vulgarizing of the individual.—You are not an individual....'
and later:

'You are libelling the Artist, by your idleness.' Also, 'Your pseudo-neediness is a sentimental indulgence.'

All this swish and clatter of insult reminds one a little of Papa Karamazoff.[10] Its outrageousness is more Russian than Anglo-Victorian, but Lewis is not a mere echo of Dostoievsky. He hustles his reader, jolts him, snarls at him in contra-distinction to Dostoievsky, who merely surrounds him with an enveloping dreariness, and imparts his characters by long-drawn osmosis.

Hobson is a minor character in the book, he and Lowndes are little more than a prologue, a dusty avenue of approach to the real business of the book; Bertha, 'high standard Aryan female, in good condition, superbly made; of the succulent, obedient, clear peasant type....'

Kreisler, the main character in the book, a 'powerful' study in sheer obsessed emotionality, the chief foil to Tarr who has, over and above his sombre emotional spawn-bed, a smouldering sort of intelligence, combustible into brilliant talk, and brilliant invective.

Anastasya, a sort of super-Bertha, designated by the author as 'swagger sex'.

These four figures move, lit by the flare of restaurants and cafés, against the frowsy background of 'Bourgeois Bohemia', more or less Bloomsbury. There are probably such Bloomsbury's in Paris and in every large city.

This sort of catalogue is not well designed to interest the general reader. What matters is the handling, the vigour, even the violence, of the handling.

The book's interest is not due to the 'style' in so far as 'style' is generally taken to mean 'smoothness of finish', orderly arrangement of sentences, coherence to the Flaubertian method.

It *is* due to the fact that we have a highly-energized mind performing a huge act of scavenging; cleaning up a great lot of rubbish, cultural, Bohemian, romantico-Tennysonish, arty, societish, gutterish.

It is not an attack on the *épicier*.[11] It is an attack on a sort of super-*épicier* desiccation. It is by no means a tract. If Hobson is so drawn as to disgust one with the 'stuffed-shirt', Kreisler is equally a sign-post pointing to the advisability of some sort of intellectual or at least commonsense management of the emotions.

Tarr is, even Kreisler is, very nearly justified by the depiction of the Bourgeois Bohemian fustiness: Fräulein Lippmann, Fräulein Fogs, etc.

What we are blessedly free from is the red-plush Wellsian illusionism, and the click of Mr Bennett's cash-register finish. The book does not skim over the surface. If it does not satisfy the mannequin demand for 'beauty' it at least refuses to accept margarine substitutes. It will not be praised by Katherine Tynan,[12] nor by Mr Chesterton[13] and Mrs Meynell.[14] It will not receive the sanction of Dr Sir Robertson Nicholl,[15] nor of his despicable paper *The Bookman*.

(There will be perhaps some hope for the British reading public, when said paper is no longer to be found in the Public Libraries of the Island, and when Clement Shorter[16] shall cease from animadverting.) *Tarr* does not appeal to these people nor to the audience which they have swaddled. Neither, of course, did Samuel Butler[17] to their equivalents in past decades.

'Bertha and Tarr took a flat in the Boulevard Port Royal, not far from the Jardin des Plantes. They gave a party to which Fräulein Lippmann and a good many other people came. He maintained the rule of four to seven, roughly, for Bertha, with the uttermost punctiliousness. Anastasya and Bertha did not meet.

Bertha's child came, and absorbed her energies for upwards of a year. It bore some resemblance to Tarr. Tarr's afternoon visits became less frequent. He lived now publicly with his illicit and splendid bride.

Two years after the birth of the child, Bertha divorced Tarr. She then married an eye-doctor, and lived with a brooding severity in his company, and that of her only child.

Tarr and Anastasya did not marry. They had no children. Tarr, however, had three children by a Lady of the name of Rose Fawcett, who consoled him eventually for the splendours of his 'perfect woman'. But yet beyond the dim though sordid figure of Rose Fawcett, another arises. This one represents the swing-back of the pendulum once more to the swagger side. The cheerless and stodgy absurdity of Rose Fawcett required the painted, fine and inquiring face of Prism Dirkes.'

Neither this well-written conclusion, nor the opening tirade I have quoted, gives the full impression of the book's vital quality, but they may perhaps draw the explorative reader.

'Tarr' finds sex a monstrosity, he finds it 'a German study'; 'Sex Hobson, is a German study. A German study.'

At that we may leave it. 'Tarr' 'Had no social machinery, but the cumbrous one of the intellect.... When he tried to be amiable he usually only succeeded in being ominous.'

'Tarr' really gets at something in his last long discussion with Anastasya, when he says that art 'has no inside'. This is a condition of art, '*to have no* inside, nothing you cannot see. It is not something impelled like a machine by a little egoistic inside.'

'Deadness, in the limited sense in which we use that word, is the first condition of art. The second is absence of *soul*, in the sentimental human sense. The lines and masses of a statue are its soul.'

Joyce says something of the sort very differently, he is full of technical scholastic terms: '*stasis, kinesis*', etc.[18] Any careful statement of this sort is bound to be *baffoué*, and fumbled over, but this ability to come to a hard definition of anything is one of Lewis' qualities lying at the base of his ability to irritate the mediocre intelligence. The book was written before 1914, and the depiction of the German was not a piece of war propaganda.

1   Lewis's illustrations to Shakespeare's *Timon of Athens*, issued by the Cube Press in 1913.
2   John Quinn (1870-1924), an American collector, bought much of Lewis's work from 1916; his collection was auctioned in 1927.
3   Now the Victoria and Albert Museum.
4   A large painting of 1914; see Walter Michel, *Wyndham Lewis. Paintings and Drawings* (1971).
5   (1854-1930), the creator of Sherlock Holmes.
6   Mrs Humphry Ward (1851-1920) was a prolific and successful novelist.
7   George Meredith (1828-1909), the Victorian novelist.
8   Mürger's *La Vie de Bohème* (1851) gave a lively account of life in the Latin Quarter of Paris; it inspired Puccini's opera *La Bohème* (1895).
9   A restaurant chain.
10 In Dostoievsky's *The Brothers Karamazov* (1880).
11 Philistine (literally, grocer).
12 (1861-1931), Irish poet and reviewer.
13 G.K. Chesterton (1874-1936), influential Roman Catholic critic.
14 Alice Meynell (1847-1922), Roman Catholic poet and critic.
15 (1851-1923), founder editor of the middle-brow journal *The Bookman*.
16 (1857-1926), middle-brow literary critic, who contributed a weekly column to *The Sphere* from 1900 to 1926.
17 Butler (1835-1902), the author of *Erewhon* (1872), *The Authoress of the Odyssey* (1897) and *The Way of All Flesh* (1903), was admired by Pound for his independence of mind.
18 See No. 9 in the present volume.

W.B. Yeats

William Butler Yeats (1865-1939) was the leading poet of his generation, and founder with Lady Gregory of the Irish National Theatre Company, which opened the Abbey Theatre in Dublin in 1904. Yeats's criticism was collected in Ideas of Good and Evil *(1903),* Discoveries *(1907),* The Cutting of an Agate *(1912; 1919),* Plays and Controversies *(1923) and* Essays *(1924).*

Norman Jeffares edited Yeats. Selected Literary Criticism *in 1964.*

12 'A People's Theatre. A Letter to Lady Gregory', 1919

First published in two issues of The Irish Statesman, *29 November and 6 December 1919; included in the section on the Irish Dramatic Movement in* Plays and Controversies *(1923). Yeats's 1923 note states: 'I took the title from a book by Romain Rolland on some French theatrical experiments. "A People's Theatre" is not quite the same thing as "A Popular Theatre".' Yeats was disappointed that the Theatre's success was built on comedies by playwrights like Lennox Robinson and St John Ervine, while his own mythological plays were not popular.*

I

My dear Lady Gregory – Of recent years you have done all that is anxious and laborious in the supervision of the Abbey Theatre and left me free to follow my own thoughts. It is therefore right that I address to you this letter, wherein I shall explain, half for your ears, half for other ears, certain thoughts that have made me believe that the Abbey Theatre can never do all we had hoped. We set out to make a 'People's Theatre', and in that we have succeeded. But I did not know until very lately that there are certain things, dear to both our hearts, which no 'People's Theatre' can accomplish. [...]

[...]

III

We have been the first to create a true 'People's Theatre', and we

79

have succeeded because it is not an exploitation of local colour, or of a limited form of drama possessing a temporary novelty, but the first doing of something for which the world is ripe, something that will be done all over the world and done more and more perfectly; the making articulate of all the dumb classes each with its own knowledge of the world, its own dignity, but all objective with the objectivity of the office and the workshop, of the newspaper and the street, of mechanism and of politics.

IV

Yet we did not set out to create this sort of theatre, and its success has been to me a discouragement and a defeat.

[. . .]

You and I and Synge,[1] not understanding the clock, set out to bring again the theatre of Shakespeare or rather perhaps of Sophocles. I had told you how at Young Ireland Societies and the like, young men when I was twenty had read papers to one another about Irish legend and history, and you yourself soon discovered the Gaelic League, then but a new weak thing, and taught yourself Irish. At Spiddal or near it an inn-keeper had sung us Gaelic songs, all new village work that though not literature had *naïveté* and sincerity. The writers, caring nothing for cleverness, had tried to express emotion, tragic or humorous, and great masterpieces, *The Grief of a Girl's Heart*,[2] for instance, had been written in the same speech and manner and were still sung. We know that the songs of the Thames boatmen, to name but these, in the age of Queen Elizabeth had the same relation to great masterpieces. These Gaelic songs were as unlike as those to the songs of the music-hall with their clever ear-catching rhythm, the work of some mind as objective as that of an inventor or of a newspaper reporter. We thought we could bring the old folk-life to Dublin, patriotic feeling to aid us, and with the folk-life all the life of the heart, understanding heart, according to Dante's definition, as the most interior being; but the modern world is more powerful than any propaganda or even than any special circumstance, and our success has been that we have made a Theatre of the head, and persuaded Dublin playgoers to think about their own trade or profession or class and their life within it, so long as the stage curtain is up, in relation to Ireland as a whole. For certain hours of an evening they have objective modern eyes.

[. . .]

VI

I want to create for myself an unpopular theatre and an audience like a secret society where admission is by favour and never to many. Perhaps I shall never create it, for you and I and Synge have had to dig the stone for our statue and I am aghast at the sight of a new quarry, and besides I want so much–an audience of fifty, a room worthy of it (some great dining-room or drawing-room), half a dozen young men and women who can dance and speak verse or play drum and flute and zither, and all the while, instead of a profession, I but offer them 'an accomplishment'. However, there are my *Four Plays for Dancers*[3] as a beginning, some masks by Mr. Dulac[4], music by Mr. Dulac and by Mr. Rummell[5]. In most towns one can find fifty people for whom one need not build all on observation and sympathy, because they read poetry for their pleasure and understand the traditional language of passion. I desire a mysterious art, always reminding and half-reminding those who understand it of dearly loved things, doing its work by suggestion, not by direct statement, a complexity of rhythm, colour, gesture, not space-pervading like the intellect, but a memory and a prophecy: a mode of drama Shelley and Keats could have used without ceasing to be themselves, and for which even Blake in the mood of *The Book of Thel*[6] might not have been too obscure. Instead of advertisements in the Press I need a hostess, and even the most accomplished hostess must choose with more than usual care, for I have noticed that city-living cultivated people, whose names would first occur to her, set great value on painting, which is a form of property, and on music, which is a part of the organisation of life, while the lovers of literature, those who read a book many times, are either young men with little means or live far away from big towns.

What alarms me most is how a new art needing so elaborate a technique can make its first experiments before those who, as Molière[7] said of the courtiers of his day, have seen so much. How shall our singers and dancers be welcomed by those who have heard Chaliapin[8] in all his parts and who know all the dances of the Russians?[9] Yet where can I find Mr. Dulac and Mr. Rummel or any to match them, but in London[10] or in Paris, and who but the leisured will welcome an elaborate art or pay for its first experiments? In one thing the luck might be upon our side. A man who loves verse and the visible arts has, in a work such as I imagined, the advantage of the professional player. The professional player becomes the amateur, the other has been preparing all his life, and certainly I shall not soon forget the rehearsal of *At the Hawk's Well*, when Mr. Ezra Pound, who had never acted on any stage, in the absence of our chief player rehearsed for half an hour. Even the forms of subjective acting that were natural to the professional stage have ceased. Where all now is sympathy and observation no Irving can carry himself with intellectual pride, nor any Salvini in half-animal nobility, both wrapped in solitude.

I know that you consider Ireland alone our business, and in that we do not differ, except that I care very little where a play of mine is first played so that it find some natural audience and good players. My rooks may sleep abroad in the fields for a while, but when the winter comes they will remember the way home to the rookery trees. Indeed, I have Ireland especially in mind, for I want to make, or to help some man some day to make, a feeling of exclusiveness, a bond among chosen spirits, a mystery almost for leisured and lettered people. Ireland has suffered more than England from democracy, for since the Wild Geese[11] fled, who might have grown to be leaders in manners and in taste, she has had but political leaders. As a drawing is defined by its outline and taste by its rejections, I too must reject and draw an outline about the thing I seek; and say that I seek, not a theatre but the theatre's anti-self, an art that can appease all within us that becomes uneasy as the curtain falls and the house breaks into applause.

VII

Meanwhile the Popular Theatre should grow always more objective; more and more a reflection of the general mind; more and more a discovery of the simple emotions that make all men kin, clearing itself the while of sentimentality, the wreckage of an obsolete popular culture, seeking always not to feel and to imagine but to understand and to see. Let those who are all personality, who can only feel and imagine, leave it, before their presence become a corruption and turn it from its honesty. The rhetoric of D'Annunzio[12], the melodrama and spectacle of the later Maeterlinck[13], are the insincerities of subjectives, who being very able men have learned to hold an audience that is not their natural audience. To be intelligible they are compelled to harden, to externalise and deform. The popular play left to itself may not lack vicissitude and development, for it may pass, though more slowly than the novel which need not carry with it so great a crowd, from the physical objectivity of Fielding and Defoe to the spiritual objectivity of Tolstoi and Dostoievsky, for beyond the whole we reach by unbiassed intellect there is another whole reached by resignation and the denial of self.

VIII

The two great energies of the world that in Shakespeare's day penetrated each other have fallen apart as speech and music fell apart at the Renaissance, and that has brought each to greater freedom, and we have to prepare a stage for the whole wealth of modern lyricism, for an art that is close to pure music, for those energies that would free the arts from imitation, that would ally acting to decoration and to the dance. We are not yet conscious, for as yet we have no philosophy, while the opposite energy is conscious. All visible history, the discoveries of science, the discussions of politics, are with it; but as I read the world, the sudden changes, or rather the sudden revelations of future changes, are not from visible history but from its anti-self. Blake says somewhere in a 'Prophetic Book' that things must complete themselves before they pass away, and every new logical development of the objective energy intensifies in an exact correspondence a counter-energy, or rather adds to an always deepening un-analysable longing. That counter-longing, having no visible past, can only become a conscious energy suddenly, in those moments of revelation which are as a flash of lightning. Are we approaching a supreme moment of self-consciousness, the two halves of the soul separate and face to face?

1   John Millington Synge (1871-1909) had been a close associate of Yeats at the Abbey Theatre, where were performed his *The Shadow of the Glen* (1903), *Riders to the Sea* (1904), *The Well of the Saints* (1905), *The Playboy of the Western World* (1907), and *The Tinker's Wedding* (1907). Both *The Shadow* and *The Playboy* aroused controversey because of their frank treatment of Irish life, which offended some Nationalists.

2   A ballad.

3   *Four Plays for Dancers* (1921) consisted of *At the Hawk's Well*, *The Only Jealousy of Emer*, *The Dreaming of the Bones* and *Calvary*.

4   Edmund Dulac (1882-1953) was closely involved with these dance-plays, providing illustrations for the 1921 edition and writing the music for *At the Hawk's Well*.

5   Walter Morse Rummell (1887-1953) was a German pianist and composer, who wrote the music for *The Only Jealousy of Emer*.

6   William Blake's *The Book of Thel* (1789).

7   Jean Baptiste Puquelin, known as Molière (1622-73), the French comic dramatist.

8   Fyodor Chaliapin (1873-1938), the great Russian bass.

9   The Russian ballet of Fokine and Diaghilev had made a great impact in Paris in 1909 and London in 1911, and continued to be a major influence.

10   Yeats's note of 1923 reads: 'I live in Dublin now, and indolence and hatred of travel will probably compel me to make my experiment there after all.'

11   Emigrés: originally Irish Jacobites who went over to the Continent on the abdication of James II in 1688.

12   Gabriele D'Annunzio (1863-1938), the Italian poet and dramatist.

13   Maurice Maeterlinck (1862-1949), Belgian Symbolist and playwright, whose plays included *Pelléas et Mélisande* (1892) and *L'Oiseau Bleu* (1909).

T.S. Eliot

Thomas Stearns Eliot (1886-1965) came to England from America, settling in 1915. He became assistant editor of The Egoist. *He published* Prufrock and Other Observations *in 1917,* Poems *in 1919, the critical volume* The Sacred Wood *in 1920,* The Waste Land, *dedicated to Ezra Pound, in 1922, and* Homage to John Dryden *in 1924. In 1922 he founded and became editor of* The Criterion.

Eliot's Selected Essays, 1917-1932 *(1932, and frequently reprinted) contains most of his important early criticism. There is a useful* Selected Prose of T.S. Eliot *(1975), edited by Frank Kermode.*

13 'Tradition and the Individual Talent', 1919

This essay, which came to be regarded as a classic exposition of Eliot's view of impersonality in poetry, was first published in The Egoist *VI, 4 (September 1919), 54-5 and VI, 5 (December 1919), 72-3.*

I

In English writing we seldom speak of tradition, though we occasionally apply its name in deploring its absence. We cannot refer to 'the tradition' or to 'a tradition'; at most, we employ the adjective in saying that the poetry of So-and-so is 'traditional' or even 'too traditional'. Seldom, perhaps, does the word appear except in a phrase of censure. If otherwise, it is vaguely approbative, with the implication, as to the work approved, of some pleasing archaeological reconstruction. You can hardly make the word agreeable to English ears without this comfortable reference to the reassuring science of archaeology.

Certainly the word is not likely to appear in our appreciations of living or dead writers. Every nation, every race, has not only its own creative, but its own critical turn of mind; and is even more oblivious of the shortcomings and limitations of its critical habits than of those of its creative genius. We know, or think we know, from the enormous mass of critical writing that has appeared in the French language the critical method or habit of the French; we only conclude (we are such unconscious people) that the French are 'more critical' than we, and sometimes even plume ourselves a little with the fact, as if the French were the less spontaneous. Perhaps they are; but we might remind ourselves that we should be none the worse for articulating what passes in our minds when we read a book and feel an emotion about it, for criticizing our own minds in their work of criticism. One of the facts that might come to light in this process is our tendency to insist, when we praise a poet, upon those aspects of his work in which he least resembles anyone else. In these aspects or parts of his work we pretend to find what is individual, what is the peculiar essence of the man. We dwell with satisfaction upon the poet's difference from his predecessors, especially his immediate predecessors; we endeavour to find something that can be isolated in order to be enjoyed. Whereas if we approach a poet without this prejudice we shall often find that not only the best, but the most individual parts of his work may be those in which the dead poets, his ancestors, assert their immortality most vigorously. And I do not mean the impressionable period of adolescence, but the period of full maturity.

Yet if the only form of tradition, of handing down, consisted in following the ways of the immediate generation before us in a blind or timid adherence to its successes, 'tradition' should positively be discouraged. We have seen many such simple currents soon lost in the sand; and novelty is better than repetition. Tradition is a matter of much wider significance. It cannot be inherited, and if you want it you must obtain it by great labour. It involves, in the first place, the historical sense, which we may call nearly indispensable to anyone who would continue to be a poet beyond his twenty-fifth year; and the historical sense involves a perception, not only of the pastness of the past, but of its presence; the historical sense compels a man to write not merely with his own generation in his bones, but with a feeling that the whole of the literature of his own country has a simultaneous existence and composes a simultaneous order. This historical sense, which is a sense of the timeless as well as of the temporal and of the timeless and of the temporal together, is what makes a writer traditional. And it is at the same time what makes a writer most acutely conscious of his place in time, of his own contemporaneity.

No poet, no artist of any art, has his complete meaning alone. His significance, his appreciation is the appreciation of his relation to the dead poets and artists. You cannot value him alone; you must set him, for contrast and comparison, among the dead. I mean this as a principle of aesthetic, not merely historical, criticism. The necessity that he shall conform, that he shall cohere, is not onesided; what happens when a new work of art is created is something that happens simultaneously to all the works of art which preceded it. The existing monuments form an ideal order among themselves, which is modified by the introduction of the new (the really new) work of art among them. The existing order is complete before the new work arrives; for order to persist after the supervention of novelty, the *whole* existing order must be, if ever so slightly, altered; and so the relations, proportions, values of each work of art toward the whole are readjusted; and this is conformity between the old and the new. Whoever has approved this idea of order, of the form of European, of English literature will not find it preposterous that the past should be altered by the present as much as the present is directed by the past. And the poet who is aware of this will be aware of great difficulties and responsibilities.

In a peculiar sense he will be aware also that he must inevitably be judged by the standards of the past. I say judged, not amputated, by them; not judged to be as good as, or worse or better than, the dead; and certainly not judged by the canons of dead critics. It is a judgment, a comparison, in which two things are measured by each other. To conform merely would be for the new work not really to conform at all; it would not be new, and would therefore not be a work of art. And we do not quite say that the new is more valuable because it fits in; but its fitting in is a test of its value – a test, it is true, which can only be slowly and cautiously applied, for we are none of us infallible judges of conformity. We say: it appears to conform, and is perhaps individual, or it appears individual, and may conform; but we are hardly likely to find that it is one and not the other.

To proceed to a more intelligible exposition of the relation of the poet to the past: he can neither take the past as a lump, an indiscriminate bolus, nor can he form himself wholly on one or two private admirations, nor can he form himself wholly upon one preferred period. The first course is inadmissible, the second is an important experience of youth, and the third is a pleasant and highly desirable supplement. The poet must be very conscious of the main current, which does not at all flow invariably through the most distinguished reputations. He must be quite aware of the obvious fact that art never improves, but that the material of art is never quite the same. He must be aware that the mind of Europe – the mind of his own country – a mind which he learns in time to be much more important than his own private mind – is a mind which changes, and that this change is a development which abandons nothing *en route*, which does not superannuate either Shakespeare, or Homer, or the rock drawing of the Magdalenian draughtsmen. That this development, refinement perhaps, complication certainly, is not, from the point of view of the artist, any improvement. Perhaps not even an improvement from the point of view of the psychologist or not to the extent which we imagine; perhaps only in the end based upon a complication in economics and machinery. But the difference between the present and the past is that the conscious present is an awareness of the past in a way and to an extent which the past's awareness of itself cannot show.

Someone said: 'The dead writers are remote from us because we *know* so much more than they did'. Precisely, and they are that which we know.

I am alive to a usual objection to what is clearly part of my programme for the *métier* of poetry. The objection is that the doctrine requires a ridiculous amount of erudition (pedantry), a claim which can be rejected by appeal to the lives of poets in any pantheon. It will even be affirmed that much learning deadens or perverts poetic sensibility. While, however, we persist in believing that a poet ought to know as much as will not encroach upon his necessary receptivity and necessary laziness, it is not desirable to confine knowledge to whatever can be put into a useful shape for examinations, drawing-rooms, or the still more pretentious modes of publicity. Some can absorb knowledge, the more tardy must sweat for it. Shakespeare acquired more essential history from Plutarch[1] than most men could from the whole British Museum. What is to be insisted upon is that the poet must develop or procure the consciousness of the past and that he should continue to develop this consciousness throughout his career.

What happens is a continual surrender of himself as he is at the moment to something which is more valuable. The progress of an artist is a continual self-sacrifice, a continual extinction of personality.

There remains to define this process of depersonalization and its relation to the sense of tradition. It is in this depersonalization that art may be said to approach the condition of science. I therefore invite you to consider, as a suggestive analogy, the action which takes place when a bit of finely filiated platinum is introduced into a chamber containing oxygen and sulphur dioxide.

II

Honest criticism and sensitive appreciation is directed not upon the poet but upon the poetry. If we attend to the confused cries of the newspaper critics and the susurrus of popular repetition that follows, we shall hear the names of poets in great numbers; if we seek not

Blue-book[2] knowledge but the enjoyment of poetry, and ask for a poem, we shall seldom find it. I have tried to point out the importance of the relation of the poem to other poems by other authors, and suggested the conception of poetry as a living whole of all the poetry that has ever been written. The other aspect of this Impersonal theory of poetry is the relation of the poem to its author. And I hinted, by an analogy, that the mind of the mature poet differs from that of the immature one not precisely in any valuation of 'personality', not being necessarily more interesting, or having 'more to say', but rather by being a more finely perfected medium in which special, or very varied, feelings are at liberty to enter into new combinations.

The analogy was that of the catalyst. When the two gases previously mentioned are mixed in the presence of a filament of platinum, they form sulphurous acid. This combination takes place only if the platinum is present; nevertheless the newly formed acid contains no trace of platinum, and the platinum itself is apparently unaffected: has remained inert, neutral, and unchanged. The mind of the poet is the shred of platinum. It may partly or exclusively operate upon the experience of the man himself; but, the more perfect the artist, the more completely separate in him will be the man who suffers and the mind which creates; the more perfectly will the mind digest and transmute the passions which are its material.

The experience, you will notice, the elements which enter the presence of the transforming catalyst, are of two kinds: emotions and feelings. The effect of a work of art upon the person who enjoys it is an experience different in kind from any experience not of art. It may be formed out of one emotion, or may be a combination of several; and various feelings, inhering for the writer in particular words or phrases or images, may be added to compose the final result. Or great poetry may be made without the direct use of any emotion whatever: composed out of feelings solely. Canto XV of the *Inferno* (Brunetto Latini) is a working up of the emotion evident in the situation; but the effect, though single as that of any work of art, is obtained by considerable complexity of detail. The last quatrain[3] gives an image, a feeling attaching to an image, which 'came', which did not develop simply out of what precedes, but which was probably in suspension in the poet's mind until the proper combination arrived for it to add itself to. The poet's mind is in fact a receptacle for seizing and storing up numberless feelings, phrases, images, which remain there until all the particles which can unite to form a new compound are present together.

If you compare several representative passages of the greatest poetry you see how great is the variety of types of combination, and also how completely any semi-ethical criterion of 'sublimity' misses the mark. For it is not the 'greatness', the intensity, of the emotions, the components, but the intensity of the artistic process, the pressure, so to speak, under which the fusion takes place, that counts. The episode of Paolo and Francesca[4] employs a definite emotion, but the intensity of the poetry is something quite different from whatever intensity in the supposed experience it may give the impression of. It is no more intense, furthermore, than Canto XXVI, the voyage of Ulysses, which has not the direct dependence upon an emotion. Great variety is possible in the process of transmutation of emotion: the murder of Agamemnon, or the agony of Othello, gives an artistic effect apparently closer to a possible original than the scenes from Dante. In the *Agamemnon*,[5] the artistic emotion approximates to the emotion of an actual spectator; in *Othello* to the emotion of the protagonist himself. But the difference between art and the event is always absolute; the combination which is the murder of Agamemnon is probably as complex as that which is the voyage of Ulysses. In either case there has been a fusion of elements. The ode of Keats contains a number of feelings which have nothing particular to do with the nightingale, but which the nightingale, partly perhaps because of its attractive name, and partly because of its reputation, served to bring together.

The point of view which I am struggling to attack is perhaps related to the metaphysical theory of the substantial unity of the soul: for my meaning is, that the poet has, not a 'personality' to express, but a particular medium, which is only a medium and not a personality, in which impressions and experiences combine in peculiar and unexpected ways. Impressions and experiences which are important for the man may take no place in the poetry, and those which become important in the poetry may play quite a negligible part in the man, the personality.

I will quote a passage which is unfamiliar enough to be regarded with fresh attention in the light–or darkness–of these observations:

> And now methinks I could e'en chide myself
> For doating on her beauty, though her death
> Shall be revenged after no common action.
> Does the silkworm expend her yellow labours
> For thee? For thee does she undo herself?
> Are lordships sold to maintain ladyships
> For the poor benefit of a bewildering minute?

Why does yon fellow falsify highways,
And put his life between the judge's lips,
To refine such a thing–keeps horse and men
To beat their valours for her? ...[6]

In this passage (as is evident if it is taken in its context) there is a combination of positive and negative emotions: an intensely strong attraction toward beauty and an equally intense fascination by the ugliness which is contrasted with it and which destroys it. This balance of contrasted emotion is in the dramatic situation to which the speech is pertinent, but that situation alone is inadequate to it. This is, so to speak, the structural emotion, provided by the drama. But the whole effect, the dominant tone, is due to the fact that a number of floating feelings, having an affinity to this emotion by no means superficially evident, have combined with it to give us a new art emotion.

It is not in his personal emotions, the emotions provoked by particular events in his life, that the poet is in any way remarkable or interesting. His particular emotions may be simple, or crude, or flat. The emotion in his poetry will be a very complex thing, but not with the complexity of the emotions of people who have very complex or unusual emotions in life. One error, in fact, of eccentricity in poetry is to seek for new human emotions to express; and in this search for novelty in the wrong place it discovers the perverse. The business of the poet is not to find new emotions, but to use the ordinary ones and, in working them up into poetry, to express feelings which are not in actual emotions at all. And emotions which he has never experienced will serve his turn as well as those familiar to him. Consequently, we must believe that 'emotion recollected in tranquillity'[7] is an inexact formula. For it is neither emotion, nor recollection, nor, without distortion of meaning, tranquillity. It is a concentration, and a new thing resulting from the concentration, of a very great number of experiences which to the practical and active person would not seem to be experiences at all; it is a concentration which does not happen consciously or of deliberation. These experiences are not 'recollected', and they finally unite in an atmosphere which is 'tranquil' only in that it is a passive attending upon the event. Of course this is not quite the whole story. There is a great deal, in the writing of poetry, which must be conscious and deliberate. In fact, the bad poet is usually unconscious where he ought to be conscious, and conscious where he ought to be unconscious. Both errors tend to make him 'personal'. Poetry is not a turning loose of emotion, but an escape from emotion; it is not the expression of personality, but an escape from personality.

But, of course, only those who have personality and emotions know what it means to want to escape from these things.

III

ὁ δὲ νοῦς ἴσως θειότερόν τι καὶ ἀπαθές ἐστιν.[8]

This essay proposes to halt at the frontier of metaphysics or mysticism, and confine itself to such practical conclusions as can be applied by the responsible person interested in poetry. To divert interest from the poet to the poetry is a laudable aim: for it would conduce to a juster estimation of actual poetry, good and bad. There are many people who appreciate the expression of sincere emotion in verse, and there is a smaller number of people who can appreciate technical excellence. But very few know when there is an expression of *significant* emotion, emotion which has its life in the poem and not in the history of the poet. The emotion of art is impersonal. And the poet cannot reach this impersonality without surrendering himself wholly to the work to be done. And he is not likely to know what is to be done unless he lives in what is not merely the present, but the present moment of the past, unless he is conscious, not of what is dead, but of what is already living.

1 Plutarch was a first-century Greek philosopher and biographer; his *Lives of the noble Grecians and Romans*, as translated by Sir Thomas North in 1579, provided Shakespeare with the source for his Roman plays.
2 Blue Books are official Parliamentary reports, primarily concerned with facts.
3 In C. H. Sisson's translation (1980), this reads:
   Then he turned back, and seemed to be one of those
   Who, at Verona, run for the green cloth,
   Through the open country; and he seemed to be the one

   Who wins the race, and not the one who loses.
4 The famous love affair is described by Dante in *Inferno*, Canto V.
5 The Greek tragedy by Aeschylus, first performed in 458 BC.
6 Cyril Tourneur (1575-1626) in *The Revenger's Tragedy* (published 1607), III, v; the speaker is Vendice.
7 The phrase is from Wordworth's Preface to *Lyrical Ballads* (1802 edition).
8 'The mind is no doubt more divine and less subject to passion.' Aristotle, *De Anima (On the Soul)*, I, 4.

14 'The Metaphysical Poets', 1921

The essay originally constituted a review of H.J.C. Grierson's Metaphysical Lyrics and Poems of the Seventeenth Century, *published in 1921. The review appeared in* The Times Literary Supplement *1031 (20 October 1921), 669-70, and in* Homage to John

Dryden *(1924). The majority of the references are to poets included in the anthology; these have not been annotated.*

By collecting these poems from the work of a generation more often named than read, and more often read than profitably studied, Professor Grierson has rendered a service of some importance. Certainly the reader will meet with many poems already preserved in other anthologies, at the same time that he discovers poems such as those of Aurelian Townshend or Lord Herbert of Cherbury here included. But the function of such an anthology as this is neither that of Professor Saintsbury's admirable edition of Caroline[1] poets nor that of the *Oxford Book of English Verse*. Mr. Grierson's book is in itself a piece of criticism, and a provocation of criticism; and we think that he was right in including so many poems of Donne, elsewhere (though not in many editions) accessible, as documents in the case of 'metaphysical poetry'. The phrase has long done duty as a term of abuse,[2] or as the label of a quaint and pleasant taste. The question is to what extent the so-called metaphysicals formed a school (in our own time we should say a 'movement'), and how far this so-called school or movement is a digression from the main current.

Not only is it extremely difficult to define metaphysical poetry, but difficult to decide what poets practise it and in which of their verses. The poetry of Donne (to whom Marvell and Bishop King are sometimes nearer than any of the other authors) is late Elizabethan, its feeling often very close to that of Chapman. The 'courtly' poetry is derivative from Jonson, who borrowed liberally from the Latin; it expires in the next century with the sentiment and witticism of Prior.[3] There is finally the devotional verse of Herbert, Vaughan, and Crashaw (echoed long after by Christina Rossetti[4] and Francis Thompson[5]); Crashaw, sometimes more profound and less sectarian than the others, has a quality which returns through the Elizabethan period to the early Italians. It is difficult to find any precise use of metaphor, simile, or other conceit, which is common to all the poets and at the same time important enough as an element of style to isolate these poets as a group. Donne, and often Cowley, employ a device which is sometimes considered characteristically 'metaphysical'; the elaboration (contrasted with the condensation) of a figure of speech to the furthest stage to which ingenuity can carry it. Thus Cowley develops the commonplace comparison of the world to a chess-board through long stanzas (*To Destiny*), and Donne, with more grace, in *A Valediction*, the comparison of two lovers to a pair of compasses. But elsewhere we find, instead of the mere explication of the content of a comparison, a development by rapid association of thought which requires considerable agility on the part of the reader.

> On a round ball
> A workeman that hath copies by, can lay
> An Europe, Afrique, and an Asia,
> And quickly make that, which was nothing, All,
> > So doth each teare,
> > Which thee doth weare,
> A globe, yea world by that impression grow,
> Till thy tears mixt with mine doe overflow
> This world, by waters sent from thee, my heaven dissolved so.

Here we find at least two connexions which are not implicit in the first figure, but are forced upon it by the poet: from the geographer's globe to the tear, and the tear to the deluge. On the other hand, some of Donne's most successful and characteristic effects are secured by brief words and sudden contrasts:

> A bracelet of bright hair about the bone,

where the most powerful effect is produced by the sudden contrast of associations of 'bright hair' and of 'bone'. This telescoping of images and multiplied associations is characteristic of the phrase of some of the dramatists of the period which Donne knew: not to mention Shakespeare, it is frequent in Middleton, Webster, and Tourneur, and is one of the sources of the vitality of their language.

Johnson, who employed the term 'metaphysical poets', apparently having Donne, Cleveland, and Cowley chiefly in mind, remarks of them that 'the most heterogeneous ideas are yoked by violence together'. The force of this impeachment lies in the failure of the conjunction, the fact that often the ideas are yoked but not united; and if we are to judge of styles of poetry by their abuse, enough examples may be found in Cleveland to justify Johnson's condemnation. But a degree of heterogeneity of material compelled into unity by the operation of the poet's mind is omnipresent in poetry. We need not select for illustration such a line as:

> Notre âme est un trois-mâts cherchant son Icarie;[6]

we may find it in some of the best lines of Johnson himself (*The Vanity of Human Wishes*):

> His fate was destined to a barren strand,
> A petty fortress, and a dubious hand;
> He left a name at which the world grew pale,
> To point a moral, or adorn a tale.

where the effect is due to a contrast of ideas, different in degree but the same in principle, as that which Johnson mildly reprehended. And in one of the finest poems of the age (a poem which could not have been written in any other age), the *Exequy* of Bishop King, the extended comparison is used with perfect success: the idea and the simile become one, in the passage in which the Bishop illustrates his impatience to see his dead wife, under the figure of a journey:

> Stay for me there; I will not faile
> To meet thee in that hollow Vale.
> And think not much of my delay;
> I am already on the way,
> And follow thee with all the speed
> Desire can make, or sorrows breed.
> Each minute is a short degree,
> And ev'ry houre a step towards thee.
> At night when I betake to rest,
> Next morn I rise nearer my West
> Of life, almost by eight houres sail,
> Than when sleep breath'd his drowsy gale....
> But heark! My Pulse, like a soft Drum
> Beats my approach, tells *Thee* I come;
> And slow howere my marches be,
> I shall at last sit down by *Thee*.

(In the last few lines there is that effect of terror which is several times attained by one of Bishop King's admirers, Edgar Poe.)[7] Again, we may justly take these quatrains from Lord Herbert's Ode, stanzas which would, we think, be immediately pronounced to be of the metaphysical school:

> So when from hence we shall be gone,
>   And be no more, nor you, nor I,
>   As one another's mystery,
> Each shall be both, yet both but one.
>
> This said, in her up-lifted face,
>   Her eyes, which did that beauty crown,
>   Were like two starrs, that having faln down,
> Look up again to find their place:
>
> While such a moveless silent peace
>   Did seize on their becalmed sense,
>   One would have thought some influence
> Their ravished spirits did possess.

There is nothing in these lines (with the possible exception of the stars, a simile not at once grasped, but lovely and justified) which fits Johnson's general observations on the metaphysical poets in his essay on Cowley. A good deal resides in the richness of association which is at the same time borrowed from and given to the word 'becalmed'; but the meaning is clear, the language simple and elegant. It is to be observed that the language of these poets is as a rule simple and pure; in the verse of George Herbert this simplicity is carried as far as it can go–a simplicity emulated without success by numerous modern poets. The *structure* of the sentences, on the other hand, is sometimes far from simple, but this is not a vice; it is a fidelity to thought and feeling. The effect, at its best, is far less artificial than that of an ode by Gray. And as this fidelity induces variety of thought and feeling, so it induces variety of music. We doubt whether, in the eighteenth century, could be found two poems in nominally the same metre, so dissimilar as Marvell's *Coy Mistress* and Crashaw's *Saint Teresa;* the one producing an effect of great speed by the use of short syllables, and the other an ecclesiastical solemnity by the use of long ones:

Love, thou art absolute sole lord
Of life and death.

If so shrewd and sensitive (though so limited) a critic as Johnson failed to define metaphysical poetry by its faults, it is worth while to inquire whether we may not have more success by adopting the opposite method: by assuming that the poets of the seventeenth century (up to the Revolution) were the direct and normal development of the precedent age; and, without prejudicing their case by the adjective 'metaphysical', consider whether their virtue was not something permanently valuable, which subsequently disappeared, but ought not to have disappeared. Johnson has hit, perhaps by accident, on one of their peculiarities, when he observes that 'their attempts were always analytic'; he would not agree that, after the dissociation, they put the material together again in a new unity.

It is certain that the dramatic verse of the later Elizabethan and early Jacobean poets expresses a degree of development of sensibility which is not found in any of the prose, good as it often is. If we except Marlowe, a man of prodigious intelligence, these dramatists were directly or indirectly (it is at least a tenable theory) affected by Montaigne. Even if we except also Jonson and Chapman, these two were notably erudite, and were notably men who incorporated their erudition into their sensibility: their mode of feeling was directly and freshly altered by their reading and thought. In Chapman especially there is a direct sensuous apprehension of thought, or a recreation of thought into feeling, which is exactly what we find in Donne:

> in this one thing, all the discipline
> Of manners and of manhood is contained;
> A man to join himself with th' Universe
> In his main sway, and make in all things fit
> One with that All, and go on, round as it;
> Not plucking from the whole his wretched part,
> And into straits, or into nought revert,
> Wishing the complete Universe might be
> Subject to such a rag of it as he;
> But to consider great Necessity.[8]

We compare this with some modern passage:

> No, when the fight begins within himself,
> A man's worth something. God stoops o' er his head,
> Satan looks up between his feet – both tug –
> He's left, himself, i' the middle; the soul wakes
> And grows. Prolong that battle through his life![9]

It is perhaps somewhat less fair, though very tempting (as both poets are concerned with the perpetuation of love by offspring), to compare with the stanzas already quoted from Lord Herbert's Ode the following from Tennyson:

> One walked between his wife and child,
> With measured footfall firm and mild,
> And now and then he gravely smiled.
> > The prudent partner of his blood
> > Leaned on him, faithful, gentle, good,
> > Wearing the rose of womanhood.
> And in their double love secure,
> The little maiden walked demure,
> Pacing with downward eyelids pure.
> > These three made unity so sweet,
> > My frozen heart began to beat,
> > Remembering its ancient heat.[10]

The difference is not a simple difference of degree between poets. It is something which had happened to the mind of England between the time of Donne or Lord Herbert of Cherbury and the time of Tennyson and Browning; it is the difference between the intellectual poet and the reflective poet. Tennyson and Browning are poets, and they think; but they do not feel their thought as immediately as the odour of a rose. A thought to Donne was an experience; it modified his sensibility. When a poet's mind is perfectly equipped for its work, it is constantly amalgamating disparate experience; the ordinary man's experience is chaotic, irregular, fragmentary. The latter falls in love, or reads Spinoza,[11] and these two experiences have nothing to do with each other, or with the noise of the typewriter or the smell of cooking; in the mind of the poet these experiences are always forming new wholes.

We may express the difference by the following theory: The poets of the seventeenth century, the successors of the dramatists of the sixteenth, possessed a mechanism of sensibility which could devour any kind of experience. They are simple, artificial, difficult, or fantastic, as their predecessors were; no less nor more than Dante, Guido Cavalcanti, Guinicelli,[12] or Cino.[13] In the seventeenth century a dissociation of sensibility set in, from which we have never recovered; and this dissociation, as is natural, was aggravated by the influence of the two most powerful poets of the century, Milton and Dryden. Each of these men performed certain poetic functions so magnificently well that the magnitude of the effect concealed the absence of others. The language went on and in some respects improved; the best verse of Collins, Gray, Johnson, and even Goldsmith satisfies some of our fastidious demands better than that of Donne or Marvell or King. But while the language became more refined, the feeling became more crude. The feeling, the sensibility, expressed in the *Country Churchyard* (to say nothing of Tennyson and Browning) is cruder than that in the *Coy Mistress*.

The second effect of the influence of Milton and Dryden followed from the first, and was therefore slow in manifestation. The sentimental age began early in the eighteenth century, and continued. The poets revolted against the ratiocinative, the descriptive; they thought and felt by fits, unbalanced; they reflected. In one or two passages of Shelley's *Triumph of Life*, in the second *Hyperion*, there are traces of a struggle toward unification of sensibility. But Keats and Shelley died, and Tennyson and Browning ruminated.

After this brief exposition of a theory–too brief, perhaps, to carry conviction–we may ask, what would have been the fate of the 'metaphysical' had the current of poetry descended in a direct line from them, as it descended in a direct line to them? They would not, certainly, be classified as metaphysical. The possible interests of a poet are unlimited; the more intelligent he is the better; the more intelligent he is the more likely that he will have interests: our only condition is that he turn them into poetry, and not merely meditate on them poetically. A philosophical theory which has entered into poetry is established, for its truth or falsity in one sense ceases to matter, and its truth in another sense is proved. The poets in question have, like other poets, various faults. But they were, at best, engaged in the task of trying to find the verbal equivalent for states of mind and feeling. And this means both that they are more mature, and that they wear better, than later poets of cetainly not less literary ability.

It is not a permanent necessity that poets should be interested in philosophy, or in any other subject. We can only say that it appears likely that poets in our civilization, as its exists at present, must be *difficult*. Our civilization comprehends great variety and complexity, and this variety and complexity, playing upon a refined sensiblity, must produce various and complex results. The poet must become more and more comprehensive, more allusive, more indirect, in order to force, to dislocate if necessary, language into his meaning. (A brilliant and extreme statement of this view, with which it is not requisite to associate oneself, is that of M. Jean Epstein, *La Poésie d'aujourd-hui*.)[14] Hence we get something which looks very much like the conceit – we get, in fact, a method curiously similar to that of the 'metaphysical poets', similar also in its use of obscure words and of simple phrasing.

> O géraniums diaphanes, guerroyeurs sortilèges,
> Sacrilèges monomanes!
> Emballages, dévergondages, douches! O pressoirs
> Des vendanges des grands soirs!
> Layettes aux abois,
> Thyrses au fond des bois!
> Transfusions, représailles,
> Relevailles, compresses et l'éternal potion,
> Angélus! n' en pouvoir plus
> De débâcles nuptiales! de débâcles nuptiales![15]

The same poet could write also simply:

> Elle est bien loin, elle pleure,
> Le grand vent se lamente aussi...[16]

Jules Laforgue, and Tristan Corbière in many of his poems, are nearer to the 'school of Donne' than any modern English poet. But poets more classical than they have the same essential quality of transmuting ideas into sensations, of transforming an observation into a state of mind.

Pour l'enfant, amoureux de cartes et d'estampes,
L'univers est égal à son vaste appétit.
Ah, que le monde est grand à la clarté des lampes!
Aux yeux du souvenir que le monde est petit![17]

In French literature the great master of the seventeenth century–Racine–and the great master of the nineteenth–Baudelaire–are in some ways more like each other than they are like anyone else. The greatest two masters of diction are also the greatest two psychologists, the most curious explorers of the soul. It is interesting to speculate whether it is not a misfortune that two of the greatest masters of diction in our language, Milton and Dryden, triumph with a dazzling disregard of the soul. If we continued to produce Miltons and Drydens it might not so much matter, but as things are it is a pity that English poetry has remained so incomplete. Those who object to the 'artificiality' of Milton or Dryden sometimes tell us to 'look into our hearts and write'.[18] But that is not looking deep enough; Racine[19] or Donne looked into a good deal more than the heart. One must look into the cerebral cortex, the nervous system, and the digestive tracts.

May we not conclude, then, that Donne, Crashaw, Vaughan, Herbert and Lord Herbert, Marvell, King, Cowley at his best, are in the direct current of English poetry, and that their faults should be reprimanded by this standard rather than coddled by antiquarian affection? They have been enough praised in terms which are implicit limitations because they are 'metaphysical' or 'witty', 'quaint' or 'obscure', though at their best they have not these attributes more than other serious poets. On the other hand, we must not reject the criticism of Johnson (a dangerous person to disagree with) without having mastered it, without having assimilated the Johnsonian canons of taste. In reading the celebrated passage in his essay on Cowley we must remember that by wit he clearly means something more serious than we usually mean to-day; in his criticism of their versification we must remember in what a narrow discipline he was trained, but also how well trained; we must remember that Johnson tortures chiefly the chief offenders, Cowley and Cleveland. It would be a fruitful work, and one requiring a substantial book, to break up the classification of Johnson (for there has been none since) and exhibit these poets in all their difference of kind and of degree, from the massive music of Donne to the faint, pleasing tinkle of Aurelian Townshend–whose *Dialogue between a Pilgrim and Time* is one of the few regrettable omissions from the excellent anthology of Professor Grierson.

1 George Saintsbury (1845-1933) edited *Minor Poets of the Caroline Period* in three volumes from 1905; the third volume appeared in 1921.

2   Dr Johnson in his 'Life of Abraham Cowley (1779) had made use of the term 'metaphysical' in criticising these seventeenth-century poets.

3   Matthew Prior (1664–1721) wrote much elegant and courtly verse.

4   Christina Rossetti (1830–94) wrote both secular and religious poetry.

5   Thompson (1859–1907) was a Roman Catholic convert, whose best-known poem was 'The Hound of Heaven' (1893).

6   'Our soul is a three-master seeking its Icaria.' Charles Baudelaire (1821–1867), from 'Le Voyage' II (1859).

7   Edgar Allan Poe (1809–49) wrote both poetry and fiction, usually with a macabre element.

8   George Chapman (1559-1634), dramatist and translator; in *The Revenge of Bussy D'Ambois* (1613), IV, i.

9   Robert Browning (1812–89) in 'Bishop Blougram's Apology', which appeared in *Men and Women* in 1855.

10 Alfred Tennyson (1809–92) in 'The Two Voices', which appeared in *The Lady of Shalott and Other Poems* in 1832.

11 Spinoza (1632–77), philosopher and author of the posthumously published *Ethics*.

12 Guido Guinizelli (1230/40–70), an important predecessor of Dante.

13 Cino da Pistoia (*c*1270–1336), admired by Dante for his love poetry.

14 Epstein's book was published in Paris in 1921.

15 Jules Laforgue, in *Derniers Vers* (1890), X:
> O diaphanous geraniums, war-like spells,
> Obsessive sacrileges!
> Wrappings, profligacies, showers! O presses
> Of the harvest of great evenings!
> Layettes in extremity,
> Thyrses deep in the moor!
> Transfusions, reprisals,
> Churchings, compresses, and the eternal potion,
> Angelus! to be capable no more
> Of nuptial débâcles! of nuptial débâcles.

16 Laforgue, 'Sur un Defunte' in the same volume:
> She is very far away, she weeps,
> The great wind laments also.

17 Baudelaire, 'Le Voyage', I:
> For the child, fond of maps and prints,
> The universe is equal to his vast appetite.
> Oh, how large the world is in the brightness of lamps!
> To the eyes of memory how small the world!

18 Adapted from Philip Sidney's *Astrophel and Stella* (1580–4), I, 14.

19 Jean Racine (1634–99), the great French dramatist.

15 'Ulysses, *Order and Myth', 1923*

This review of Joyce's Ulysses *appeared in* The Dial *LXXV, 5 (November 1923), 480-3. The criticism by Richard Aldington which Eliot discusses had appeared in* The English Review *(April 1921), and was included in Aldington's* Literary Studies and Reviews *(1924).*

Mr. Joyce's book has been out long enough for no more general expression of praise, or expostulation with its detractors, to be necessary; and it has not been out long enough for any attempt at a complete measurement of its place and significance to be possible. All that one can usefully do at this time, and it is a great deal to do, for such a book, is to elucidate any aspect of the book–and the number of aspects is indefinite–which has not yet been fixed. I hold this book to be the most important expression which the present age has found; it is a book to which we are all indebted, and from which none of us can escape. These are postulates for anything that I have to say about it, and I have no wish to waste the reader's time by elaborating my eulogies; it has given me all the surprise, delight, and terror that I can require, and I will leave it at that.

Among all the criticisms I have seen of this book, I have seen nothing–unless we except, in its way, M. Valéry Larbaud's valuable paper which is rather an Introduction than a criticism–which seemed to me to appreciate the significance of the method employed–the parallel to the *Odyssey*, and the use of the appropriate styles and symbols to each division. Yet one might expect this to be the first peculiarity to attract attention; but it has been treated as an amusing dodge, or scaffolding erected by the author for the purpose of disposing his realistic tale, of no interest in the completed structure. The criticism which Mr. Aldington directed upon *Ulysses* several years ago seems to me to fail by this oversight–but, as Mr. Aldington wrote before the complete work had appeared, fails more honorably than the attempts of those who had the whole book before them. Mr. Aldington treated Mr. Joyce as a prophet of chaos; and wailed at the flood of Dadaism[1] which his prescient eye saw bursting forth at the tap of the magician's rod. Of course, the influence which Mr. Joyce's book may have is from my point of view an irrelevance. A very great book may have a very bad influence indeed; and a mediocre book may be in the event most salutary. The next generation is responsible for its own soul; a man of genius is responsible to his peers, not to a studio full of uneducated and undisciplined coxcombs. Still, Mr. Aldington's pathetic solicitude for the half-witted seems to me to carry certain implications about the nature of the book itself to which I cannot assent; and this is the important issue. He finds the book, if I understand him, to be an invitation to chaos, and an expression of feelings which are perverse, partial, and a distortion of reality. But unless I quote Mr. Aldington's words I am likely to falsify. 'I say, moreover,' he says, 'that when Mr. Joyce, with his marvellous gifts, uses them to disgust us with mankind, he is doing something which is false and a libel on humanity.' It is somewhat similar to the opinion of the urbane Thackeray upon Swift.[2] 'As for the moral, I think it horrible, shameful, unmanly, blasphemous: and giant and great as this Dean is, I say we should hoot him.' (This, of the conclusion of the Voyage to the Houyhnhnms–which seems to me one of the greatest triumphs that the human soul has ever achieved.–It is true that Thackeray later pays Swift one of the finest tributes that a man has ever given or received: 'So great a man he seems to me that thinking of him is like thinking of an empire falling.' And Mr. Aldington, in his time, is almost equally generous.)

Whether it is possible to libel humanity (in distinction to libel in the usual sense, which is libeling an individual or a group in contrast with the rest of humanity) is a question for philosophical societies to discuss; but of course if *Ulysses* were a 'libel' it would simply be a forged document, a powerless fraud, which would never have extracted from Mr. Aldington a moment's attention. I do not wish to linger over this point: the interesting question is that begged by Mr. Aldington when he refers to Mr. Joyce's 'great *undisciplined* talent.'

I think that Mr. Aldington and I are more or less agreed as to what we want in principle, and agreed to call it classicism. It is because of this agreement that I have chosen Mr. Aldington to attack on the present issue. We are agreed as to what we want, but not as to how to get it, or as to what contemporary writing exhibits a tendency in that direction. We agree, I hope, that 'classicism' is not an alternative to 'romanticism,' as of political parties, Conservative and Liberal, Republican and Democrat, on a 'turn-the-rascals-out' platform. It is a goal toward which all good literature strives, so far as it is good, according to the possibilities of its place and time. One can be 'classical,' in a sense, by turning away from nine-tenths of the material which lies at hand and selecting only mummified stuff from a museum–like some contemporary writers, about whom one could say some nasty things in this connection, if it were worth while (Mr. Aldington is not one of them). Or one can be classical in tendency by doing the best one can with the material at hand. The confusion springs from the fact that the term is applied to literature and to the whole complex of interests and modes of behavior and society of which literature is a part; and it has not the same bearing in both applications. It is much easier to be a classicist in literary criticism than in creative art–because in criticism you are responsible only for what you want, and in creation you are responsible for what you can do with material which you must simply accept. And in this material I include the emotions and feelings of the writer himself, which, for that writer, are simply material which he must accept–not virtues to be enlarged or vices to be diminished. The question, then, about Mr. Joyce, is: how much living material does he deal with, and how does he deal with it: deal with, not as a legislator or exhorter, but as an artist?

It is here that Mr. Joyce's parallel use of the *Odyssey* has a great importance. It has the importance of a scientific discovery. No one else has built a novel upon such a foundation before: it has never before been necessary. I am not begging the question in calling *Ulysses* a 'novel'; and if you call it an epic it will not matter. If it is not a novel, that is simply because the novel is a form which will no longer serve; it is because the novel, instead of being a form, was simply the expression of an age which had not sufficiently lost all form to feel the need of something stricter. Mr. Joyce has written one novel–the *Portrait;* Mr. Wyndham Lewis has written one novel–*Tarr.* I do not suppose that either of them will ever write another 'novel.' The novel ended with Flaubert and with James. It is, I think, because Mr. Joyce and Mr. Lewis, being 'in advance' of their time, felt a conscious or probably unconscious dissatisfaction with the form, that their novels are more formless than those of a dozen clever writers who are unaware of its obsolescence.

In using the myth, in manipulating a continuous parallel between contemporaneity and antiquity, Mr. Joyce is pursuing a method which others must pursue after him. They will not be imitators, any more than the scientist who uses the discoveries of an Einstein in pursuing his own, independent, further investigations. It is simply a way of controlling, of ordering, of giving a shape and a significance to the immense panorama of futility and anarchy which is contemporary history. It is a method already adumbrated by Mr. Yeats, and of the need for which I believe Mr. Yeats to have been the first contemporary to be conscious. It is a method for which the horoscope is auspicious. Psychology (such as it is, and whether our reaction to it be comic or serious), ethnology,[3] and *The Golden Bough*[4] have concurred to make possible what was impossible even a few years ago. Instead of narrative method, we may now use the mythical method. It is, I seriously believe, a step toward making the modern world possible for art, toward that order and form which Mr. Aldington so earnestly desires. And only those who have won their own discipline in secret and without aid, in a world which offers very little assistance to that end, can be of any use in furthering this advance.

1 The Dada movement, originating in Zürich around 1916 and lively in Paris in the 1920s, aimed to destroy sense and order in the name of

spontaneity and vitality.
2 William Makepeace Thackeray (1811-63), the Victorian novelist, attacked Swift's inhumanity in *English Humourists of the Eighteenth Century* in 1851.
3 The study of races and peoples.
4 Sir James Frazer (1854-1941) published his great work of anthropology between 1890 and 1915; Eliot refers to it in his Notes to *The Waste Land*.

Virginia Woolf

Virginia Woolf (1882-1941) began her novel-writing in a form deriving from James with The Voyage Out *(1915) and* Night and Day *(1919), but subsequently developed a more subtle Modernist technique in* Jacob's Room *(1922),* Mrs. Dalloway *(1925) and* To the Lighthouse *(1927). Her criticism first appeared as* The Common Reader: First Series *in 1925, with a* Second Series *in 1932; her feminist* A Room of One's Own *was published in 1929.*

Her literary essays constitute the first two volumes of the Collected Essays *of 1966.*

16. 'Modern Fiction', 1919
First published as 'Modern Novels' in the Times Literary Supplement *(10 April 1919), 189-90; revised and retitled for inclusion in* The Common Reader *(1925).*

In making any survey, even the freest and loosest, of modern fiction, it is difficult not to take it for granted that the modern practice of the art is somehow an improvement upon the old. With their simple tools and primitive materials, it might be said, Fielding did well and Jane Austen even better, but compare their opportunities with ours! Their masterpieces certainly have a strange air of simplicity. And yet the analogy between literature and the process, to choose an example, of making motor cars scarcely holds good beyond the first glance. It is doubtful whether in the course of the centuries, though we have learnt much about making machines, we have learnt anything about making literature. We do not come to write better; all that we can be said to do is to keep moving, now a little in this direction, now in that, but with a circular tendency should the whole course of the track be viewed from a sufficiently lofty pinnacle. It need scarcely be said that we make no claim to stand, even momentarily, upon that vantage ground. On the flat, in the crowd, half blind with dust, we look back with envy to those happier warriors, whose battle is won and whose achievements wear so serene an air of accomplishment that we can scarcely refrain from whispering that the fight was not so fierce for them as for us. It is for the historian of literature to decide; for him to say if we are now beginning or ending or standing in the middle of a great period of prose fiction, for down in the plain little is visible. We only know that certain gratitudes and hostilities inspire us; that certain paths seem to lead to fertile land, others to the dust and the desert; and of this perhaps it may be worth while to attempt some account.

Our quarrel, then, is not with the classics, and if we speak of quarrelling with Mr. Wells, Mr. Bennett, and Mr. Galsworthy, it is partly that by the mere fact of their existence in the flesh their work has a living, breathing, everyday imperfection which bids us take what liberties with it we choose. But it is also true that, while we thank them for a thousand gifts, we reserve our unconditional gratitude for Mr. Hardy, for Mr. Conrad, and in a much lesser degree for the Mr. Hudson of *The Purple Land, Green Mansions,* and *Far Away and Long Ago.*[1] Mr. Wells, Mr. Bennett, and Mr. Galsworthy have excited so many hopes and disappointed them so persistently that our gratitude largely takes the form of thanking them for having shown us what they might have done but have not done; what we certainly could not do, but as certainly, perhaps, do not wish to do. No single phrase will sum up the charge or grievance which we have to bring against a mass of work so large in its volume and embodying so many qualities, both admirable and the reverse. If we tried to formulate our meaning in one word we should say that these three writers are materialists. It is because they are concerned not with the spirit but with the body that they have disappointed us, and left us with the feeling that the sooner English fiction turns its back upon them, as politely as may be, and marches, if only into the desert, the better for its soul. Naturally, no single word reaches the centre of three separate targets. In the case of Mr. Wells it falls notably wide of the mark. And yet even with him it indicates to our thinking the fatal alloy in his genius, the great clod of clay that has got itself mixed up with the purity of his inspiration. But Mr. Bennett is perhaps the worst culprit of the three, inasmuch as he is by far the best workman. He can make a book so well constructed and solid in its craftsmanship that it is difficult for the most exacting of critics to see through what chink or crevice decay can creep in. There is not so much as a draught between the frames of the windows, or a crack in the boards. And yet – if life should refuse to live there? That is a risk which the creator of *The Old Wives' Tale*, George Cannon, Edwin Clayhanger, and hosts of other figures, may well claim to have surmounted. His characters live abundantly, even unexpectedly, but it remains to ask how do they live, and what do they live for? More and more they seem to us, deserting even the well-built villa in the Five Towns, to spend their time in some softly padded first-class railway carriage, pressing bells and buttons innumerable; and the destiny to which they travel so luxuriously becomes more and more unquestionably an eternity of bliss spent in the very best hotel in Brighton. It can scarcely be said of Mr. Wells that he is a materialist in the sense that he takes too much delight in the solidity of his fabric. His mind is too generous in its sympathies to allow him to spend much time in making things shipshape and substantial. He is a materialist from sheer goodness of heart, taking upon his shoulders the work that ought to have been discharged by Government officials, and in the plethora of his ideas and facts scarcely having leisure to realise, or forgetting to think important, the crudity and coarseness of his human beings. Yet what more damaging criticism can there be both of his earth and of his Heaven than that they are to be inhabited here and hereafter by his Joans and his Peters?[2] Does not the inferiority of their natures tarnish whatever institutions and ideals may be provided for them by the generosity of their creator? Nor, profoundly though we respect the integrity and humanity of Mr. Galsworthy, shall we find what we seek in his pages.

If we fasten, then, one label on all these books, on which is one word materialists, we mean by it that they write of unimportant things; that they spend immense skill and immense industry making the trivial and the transitory appear the true and the enduring.

We have to admit that we are exacting, and, further, that we find it difficult to justify our discontent by explaining what it is that we exact. We frame our question differently at different times. But it reappears most persistently as we drop the finished novel on the crest of a sigh—Is it worth while? What is the point of it all? Can it be that, owing to one of those little deviations which the human spirit seems to make from time to time, Mr. Bennett has come down with his magnificent apparatus for catching life just an inch or two on the wrong side? Life escapes; and perhaps without life nothing else is worth while. It is a confession of vagueness to have to make use of such a figure as this, but we scarcely better the matter by speaking, as critics are prone to do, of reality. Admitting the vagueness which afflicts all criticism of novels, let us hazard the opinion that for us at this moment the form of fiction most in vogue more often misses than secures the thing we seek. Whether we call it life or spirit, truth or reality, this, the essential thing, has moved off, or on, and refuses to be contained any longer in such ill-fitting vestments as we provide. Nevertheless, we go on perseveringly, conscientiously, constructing our two and thirty chapters after a design which more and more ceases to resemble the vision in our minds. So much of the enormous labour of proving the solidity, the likeness to life, of the story is not merely labour thrown away but labour misplaced to the extent of obscuring and blotting out the light of the conception. The writer seems constrained, not by his own free will but by some powerful and unscrupulous tyrant who has him in thrall, to provide a plot, to provide comedy, tragedy, love interest, and an air of probability embalming the whole so impeccable that if all his figures were to come to life they would find themselves dressed down to the last button of their coats in the fashion of the hour. The tyrant is obeyed; the novel is done to a turn. But sometimes, more and more often as time goes by, we suspect a momentary doubt, a spasm of rebellion, as the pages fill themselves in the customary way. Is life like this? Must novels be like this?

Look within and life, it seems, is very far from being 'like this'. Examine for a moment an ordinary mind on an ordinary day. The mind receives a myriad impressions–trivial, fantastic, evanescent, or engraved with the sharpness of steel. From all sides they come, an incessant shower of innumerable atoms; and as they fall, as they shape themselves into the life of Monday or Tuesday, the accent falls differently from of old; the moment of importance came not here but there; so that, if a writer were a free man and not a slave, if he could write what he chose, not what he must, if he could base his work upon his own feeling and not upon convention, there would be no plot, no comedy, no tragedy, no love interest or catastrophe in the accepted style, and perhaps not a single button sewn on as the Bond Street tailors would have it. Life is not a series of gig lamps[3] symmetrically arranged; life is a luminous halo, a semi-transparent envelope surrounding us from the beginning of consciousness to the end. Is it not the task of the novelist to convey this varying, this unknown and uncircumscribed spirit, whatever aberration or complexity it may display, with as little mixture of the alien and external as possible? We are not pleading merely for courage and sincerity; we are suggesting that the proper stuff of fiction is a little other than custom would have us believe it.

It is, at any rate, in some such fashion as this that we seek to define the quality which distinguishes the work of several young writers, among whom Mr. James Joyce is the most notable, from that of their predecessors. They attempt to come closer to life, and to preserve more sincerely and exactly what interests and moves them, even if to do so they must discard most of the conventions which are commonly observed by the novelist. Let us record the atoms as they fall upon the mind in the order in which they fall, let us trace the pattern, however disconnected and incoherent in appearance, which each sight or incident scores upon the consciousness. Let us not take it for granted that life exists more fully in what is commonly thought big than in what is commonly thought small. Any one who has read *The Portrait of the Artist as a Young Man* or, what promises to be a far more interesting work, *Ulysses*, now appearing in the *Little Review*, will have hazarded some theory of this nature as to Mr. Joyce's intention. On our part, with such a fragment before us, it is hazarded rather than affirmed; but whatever the intention of the whole, there can be no question but that it is of the utmost sincerity and that the result, difficult or unpleasant as we may judge it, is undeniably important. In contrast with those whom we have called materialists, Mr. Joyce is spiritual; he is concerned at all costs to reveal the flickerings of that innermost flame which flashes its messages through the brain, and in order to preserve it he disregards with complete courage whatever seems to him adventitious, whether it be probability, or coherence, or any other of these signposts which for generations have served to support the imagination of a reader when called upon to imagine what he can neither touch nor see. The scene in the cemetery, for instance, with its brilliancy, its sordidity, its incoherence, its sudden lightning flashes of significance, does undoubtedly come so close to the quick of the mind that, on a first reading at any rate, it is difficult not to acclaim a masterpiece. If we want life itself, here surely we have it. Indeed, we find ourselves fumbling rather awkwardly if we try to say what else we wish, and for what reason a work of such originality yet fails to compare, for we must take high examples, with *Youth*[4] or *The Mayor of Casterbridge*.[5] It fails because of the comparative poverty of the writer's mind, we might say simply and have done with it. But it is possible to press a little further and wonder whether we may not refer our sense of being in a bright yet narrow room, confined and shut in, rather than enlarged and set free, to some limitation imposed by the method as well as by the mind. Is it the method that inhibits the creative power? Is it due to the method that we feel neither jovial nor magnanimous, but centred in a self which, in spite of its tremor of susceptibility, never embraces or creates what is outside itself and beyond? Does the emphasis laid, perhaps didactically, upon indecency, contribute to the effect of something angular and isolated? Or is it merely that in any effort of such originality it is much easier, for contemporaries especially, to feel what it lacks than to name what it gives? In any case it is a mistake to stand outside examining 'methods'. Any method is right, every method is right, that expresses what we wish to express, if we are writers; that brings us closer to the novelist's intention if we are readers. This method has the merit of bringing us closer to what we were prepared to call life itself; did not the reading of *Ulysses* suggest how much of life is excluded or ignored, and did it not come with a shock to open *Tristram Shandy*[6] or even *Pendennis*[7] and be by them convinced that there are not only other aspects of life, but more important ones into the bargain.

However this may be, the problem before the novelist at present, as we suppose it to have been in the past, is to contrive means of being free to set down what he chooses. He has to have the courage to say that what interests him is no longer 'this' but 'that': out of 'that' alone must he construct his work. For the moderns 'that', the point of interest, lies very likely in the dark places of psychology. At once, therefore, the accent falls a little differently; the emphasis is upon something hitherto ignored; at once a different outline of form becomes necessary, difficult for us to grasp, incomprehensible to our predecessors. No one but a modern, no one perhaps but a Russian, would have felt the interest of the situation which Tchekov has made into the short story which he calls 'Gusev'[8]. Some Russian soldiers lie ill on board a ship which is taking them back to Russia. We are given a few scraps of their talk and some of their thoughts; then one of them dies and is carried away; the talk goes on among the others for a time, until Gusev himself dies, and looking 'like a carrot or a radish' is thrown overboard. The emphasis is laid upon such unexpected places that at first it seems as if there were no emphasis at all; and then, as the eyes accustom themselves to twilight and discern the shapes of things in a room we see how complete the story is, how profound, and how truly in obedience to his vision Tchekov has chosen this, that, and the other, and placed them together to compose something new. But it is impossible to say 'this is comic', or 'that is tragic', nor are we certain, since short stories, we have been taught, should be brief and conclusive, whether this, which is vague and inconclusive, should be called a short story at all.

The most elementary remarks upon modern English fiction can hardly avoid some mention of the Russian influence, and if the Russians are mentioned one runs the risk of feeling that to write of any fiction save theirs is waste of time. If we want understanding of the soul and heart where else shall we find it of comparable profundity? If we are sick of our own materialism the least considerable of their novelists has by right of birth a natural reverence for the human spirit. 'Learn to make yourself akin to people.... But let this sympathy be not with the mind–for it is easy with the mind–but with the heart, with love towards them'. In every great Russian writer we seem to discern the features of a saint, if sympathy for the sufferings of others, love towards them, endeavour to reach some goal worthy of the most exacting demands of the spirit constitute saintliness. It is the saint in them which confounds us with a feeling of our own irreligious triviality, and turns so many of our famous novels to tinsel and trickery. The conclusions of the Russian mind, thus comprehensive and compassionate, are inevitably, perhaps, of the utmost sadness. More accurately indeed we might speak of the inconclusiveness of the Russian mind. It is the sense that there is no answer, that if honestly examined life presents question after question which must be left to sound on and on after the story is over in hopeless interrogation that fills us with a deep, and finally it may be with a resentful, despair. They are right perhaps; unquestionably they see further than we do and without our gross impediments of vision. But perhaps we see something that escapes them, or why should this voice of protest mix itself with our gloom? The voice of protest is the voice of another and an ancient civilisation which seems to have bred in us the instinct to enjoy and fight rather than to suffer and understand. English fiction from Sterne to Meredith bears witness to our natural delight in humour and comedy, in the beauty of earth, in the activities of the intellect, and in the splendour of the body. But any deductions that we may draw from the comparison of two fictions so immeasurably far apart are futile save indeed as they flood us with a view of the infinite possibilities of the art and remind us that there is no limit to the horizon, and that nothing–no 'method', no experiment, even of the wildest–is forbidden, but only falsity and pretence. 'The proper stuff of fiction' does not exist; everything is the proper stuff of fiction, every feeling, every thought, every quality of brain and spirit is drawn upon; no perception comes amiss. And if we can imagine the art of fiction come alive and standing in our midst, she would undoubtedly bid us break her and bully her, as well as honour and love her, for so her youth is renewed and her sovereignty assured.

1   William Henry Hudson (1841-1922) came to England from Argentina in 1869; his works include *The Purple Land* (1885), *Green Mansions* (1904) and the autobiographical *Far Away and Long Ago* (1918).
2   Wells had published the novel *Joan and Peter* in 1918.
3   Carriage-lamps.
4   By Conrad (1902).
5   By Hardy (1886).

6 By Sterne (1760-7).
7 By Thackeray (1848).
8 In the *Oxford Chekhov*, by R. Hingley, Vol. V (1970).

17 'Mr. Bennett and Mrs. Brown', 1924

This was originally read as a paper to the Heretics at Cambridge on 18 May 1924. A version entitled 'Character in Fiction' was published in The Criterion II, *8 (July 1924) 409-30, and the revised version as a pamphlet at the Hogarth Press in 1924.*

It seems to be possible, perhaps desirable, that I may be the only person in this room who has committed the folly of writing, trying to write, or failing to write, a novel. And when I asked myself, as your invitation to speak to you about modern fiction made me ask myself, what demon whispered in my ear and urged me to my doom, a little figure rose before me–the figure of a man, or of a woman, who said, 'My name is Brown. Catch me if you can.'

Most novelists have the same experience. Some Brown, Smith, or Jones comes before them and says in the most seductive and charming way in the world, 'Come and catch me if you can.' And so, led on by this will-o'-the-wisp, they flounder through volume after volume, spending the best years of their lives in the pursuit, and receiving for the most part very little cash in exchange. Few catch the phantom; most have to be content with a scrap of her dress or a wisp of her hair.

My belief that men and women write novels because they are lured on to create some character which has thus imposed itself upon them has the sanction of Mr. Arnold Bennett. In an article from which I will quote[1] he says, 'The foundation of good fiction is character-creating and nothing else.... Style counts; plot counts; originality of outlook counts. But none of these counts anything like so much as the convincingness of the characters. If the characters are real the novel will have a chance; if they are not, oblivion will be its portion....' And he goes on to draw the conclusion that we have no young novelists of first-rate importance at the present moment, because they are unable to create characters that are real, true, and convincing.

These are the questions that I want with greater boldness than discretion to discuss tonight. I want to make out what we mean when we talk about 'character' in fiction; to say something about the question of reality which Mr. Bennett raises; and to suggest some reasons why the younger novelists fail to create characters, if, as Mr. Bennett asserts, it is true that fail they do. This will lead me, I am well aware, to make some very sweeping and some very vague assertions. For the question is an extremely difficult one. Think how little we know about character–think how little we know about art. But, to make a clearance before I begin, I will suggest that we range Edwardians and Georgians into two camps; Mr. Wells, Mr. Bennett, and Mr. Galsworthy I will call the Edwardians; Mr. Forster, Mr. Lawrence, Mr. Strachey, Mr. Joyce, and Mr. Eliot I will call the Georgians. And if I speak in the first person, with intolerable egotism, I will ask you to excuse me. I do not want to attribute to the world at large the opinions of one solitary, ill-informed, and misguided individual.

My first assertion is one that I think you will grant–that everyone in this room is a judge of character. Indeed it would be impossible to live for a year without disaster unless one practised character-reading and had some skill in the art. Our marriages, our friendships depend on it; our business largely depends on it; every day questions arise which can only be solved by its help. And now I will hazard a second assertion, which is more disputable perhaps, to the effect that in or about December, 1910, human character changed.

I am not saying that one went out, as one might into a garden, and there saw that a rose had flowered, or that a hen had laid an egg. The change was not sudden and definite like that. But a change there was, nevertheless; and, since one must be arbitrary, let us date it about the year 1910. The first signs of it are recorded in the books of Samuel Butler, in *The Way of All Flesh* in particular;[2] the plays of Bernard Shaw continue to record it. In life one can see the change, if I may use a homely illustration, in the character of one's cook. The Victorian cook lived like a leviathan in the lower depths, formidable, silent, obscure, inscrutable; the Georgian cook is a creature of sunshine and fresh air; in and out of the drawing-room, now to borrow the *Daily Herald*,[3] now to ask advice about a hat. Do you ask for more solemn instances of the power of the human race to change? Read the *Agamemnon*, and see whether, in process of time, your sympathies are not almost entirely with Clytemnestra. Or consider the married life of the Carlyles and bewail the waste, the futility, for him and for her, of the horrible domestic tradition which made it seemly for a woman of genius to spend her time chasing beetles, scouring saucepans, instead of writing books.[4] All human relations have shifted–those between masters and servants, husbands and wives, parents and children. And when human relations change there is at the same time a change in religion, conduct, politics, and literature. Let us agree to place one of these changes about the year 1910.

113

I have said that people have to acquire a good deal of skill in character-reading if they are to live a single year of life without disaster. But it is the art of the young. In middle age and in old age the art is practised mostly for its uses, and friendships and other adventures and experiments in the art of reading character are seldom made. But novelists differ from the rest of the world because they do not cease to be interested in character when they have learnt enough about it for practical purposes. They go a step further, they feel that there is something permanently interesting in character in itself. When all the practical business of life has been discharged, there is something about people which continues to seem to them of overwhelming importance, in spite of the fact that it has no bearing whatever upon their happiness, comfort, or income. The study of character becomes to them an absorbing pursuit; to impart character an obsession. And this I find it very difficult to explain: what novelists mean when they talk about character, what the impulse is that urges them so powerfully every now and then to embody their view in writing.

So, if you will allow me, instead of analysing and abstracting, I will tell you a simple story which, however pointless, has the merit of being true, of a journey from Richmond to Waterloo, in the hope that I may show you what I mean by character in itself; that you may realize the different aspects it can wear; and the hideous perils that beset you directly you try to describe it in words.

One night some weeks ago, then, I was late for the train and jumped into the first carriage I came to. As I sat down I had the strange and uncomfortable feeling that I was interrupting a conversation between two people who were already sitting there. Not that they were young or happy. Far from it. They were both elderly, the woman over sixty, the man well over forty. They were sitting opposite each other, and the man, who had been leaning over and talking emphatically to judge by his attitude and the flush on his face, sat back and became silent. I had disturbed him, and he was annoyed. The elderly lady, however, whom I will call Mrs. Brown, seemed rather relieved. She was one of those clean, threadbare old ladies whose extreme tidiness—everything buttoned, fastened, tied together, mended and brushed up—suggests more extreme poverty than rags and dirt. There was something pinched about her—a look of suffering, of apprehension, and, in addition, she was extremely small. Her feet, in their clean little boots, scarcely touched the floor. I felt she had nobody to support her; that she had to make up her mind for herself; that, having been deserted, or left a widow, years ago, she had led an anxious, harried life, bringing up an only son, perhaps, who, as likely as not, was by this time beginning to go to the bad. All this shot through my mind as I sat down, being uncomfortable, like most people, at travelling with fellow passengers unless I have somehow or other accounted for them. Then I looked at the man. He was no relation of Mrs. Brown's I felt sure; he was of a bigger, burlier, less refined type. He was a man of business I imagined, very likely a respectable corn-chandler from the North, dressed in good blue serge with a pocket-knife and a silk handerchief, and a stout leather bag. Obviously, however, he had an unpleasant business to settle with Mrs. Brown; a secret, perhaps sinister business, which they did not intend to discuss in my presence.

'Yes, the Crofts have had very bad luck with their servants,' Mr. Smith (as I will call him) said in a considering way, going back to some earlier topic, with a view to keeping up appearances.

'Ah, poor people,' said Mrs. Brown, a trifle condescendingly. 'My grandmother had a maid who came when she was fifteen and stayed till she was eighty' (this was said with a kind of hurt and aggressive pride to impress us both perhaps).

'One doesn't often come across that sort of thing nowadays,' said Mr. Smith in conciliatory tones.

Then they were silent.

'It's odd they don't start a golf club there – I should have thought one of the young fellows would,' said Mr. Smith, for the silence obviously made him uneasy.

Mrs. Brown hardly took the trouble to answer.

'What changes they're making in this part of the world,' said Mr. Smith looking out of the window, and looking furtively at me as he did so.

It was plain, from Mrs. Brown's silence, from the uneasy affability with which Mr. Smith spoke, that he had some power over her which he was exerting disagreeably. It might have been her son's downfall, or some painful episode in her past life, or her daughter's. Perhaps she was going to London to sign some document to make over some property. Obviously against her will she was in Mr. Smith's hands. I was beginning to feel a great deal of pity for her, when she said, suddenly and inconsequently:

'Can you tell me if an oak-tree dies when the leaves have been eaten for two years in succession by caterpillars?'

She spoke quite brightly, and rather precisely, in a cultivated, inquisitive voice.

Mr. Smith was startled, but relieved to have a safe topic of conversation given him. He told her a great deal very quickly about plagues of insects. He told her that he had a brother who kept a fruit farm in Kent. He told her what fruit farmers do every year in Kent, and so on, and so on. While he talked a very odd thing happened. Mrs. Brown took out her little white handkerchief and began to dab her eyes. She was crying. But she went on listening quite composedly to what he was saying, and he went on talking, a little louder, a little angrily, as if he had seen her cry often before; as if it were a painful habit. At last it got on his nerves. He stopped abruptly, looked out of the window, then leant towards her as he had been doing when I got in, and said in a bullying, menacing way, as if he would not stand any more nonsense:

'So about that matter we were discussing. It'll be all right? George will be there on Tuesday?'

'We shan't be late,' said Mrs. Brown, gathering herself together with superb dignity.

Mr. Smith said nothing. He got up, buttoned his coat, reached his bag down, and jumped out of the train before it had stopped at Clapham Junction. He had got what he wanted, but he was ashamed of himself; he was glad to get out of the old lady's sight.

Mrs. Brown and I were left alone together. She sat in her corner opposite, very clean, very small, rather queer, and suffering intensely. The impression she made was overwhelming. It came pouring out like a draught, like a smell of burning. What was it composed of–that overwhelming and peculiar impression? Myriads of irrelevant and incongruous ideas crowd into one's head on such occasions; one sees the person, one sees Mrs. Brown, in the centre of all sorts of different scenes. I thought of her in a seaside house, among queer ornaments: sea-urchins, models of ships in glass cases. Her husband's medals were on the mantelpiece. She popped in and out of the room, perching on the edges of chairs, picking meals out of saucers, indulging in long, silent stares. The caterpillars and the oak-trees seemed to imply all that. And then, into this fantastic and secluded life, in broke Mr. Smith. I saw him blowing in, so to speak, on a windy day. He banged, he slammed. His dripping umbrella made a pool in the hall. They sat closeted together.

And then Mrs. Brown faced the dreadful revelation. She took her heroic decision. Early, before dawn, she packed her bag and carried it herself to the station. She would not let Smith touch it. She was wounded in her pride, unmoored from her anchorage; she came of gentlefolks who kept servants–but details could wait. The important thing was to realize her character, to steep oneself in her atmosphere. I had no time to explain why I felt it somewhat tragic, heroic, yet with a dash of the flighty, and fantastic, before the train stopped, and I watched her disappear, carrying her bag, into the vast blazing station. She looked very small, very tenacious; at once very frail and very heroic. And I have never seen her again, and I shall never know what became of her.

The story ends without any point to it. But I have not told you this anecdote to illustrate either my own ingenuity or the pleasure of travelling from Richmond to Waterloo. What I want you to see in it is this. Here is a character imposing itself upon another person. Here is Mrs. Brown making someone begin almost automatically to write a novel about her. I believe that all novels begin with an old lady in the corner opposite. I believe that all novels, that is to say, deal with character, and that it is to express character—not to preach doctrines, sing songs, or celebrate the glories of the British Empire, that the form of the novel, so clumsy, verbose, and undramatic, so rich, elastic, and alive, has been evolved. To express character, I have said; but you will at once reflect that the very widest interpretation can be put upon those words. For example, old Mrs. Brown's character will strike you very differently according to the age and country in which you happen to be born. It would be easy enough to write three different versions of that incident in the train, an English, a French, and a Russian. The English writer would make the old lady into a 'character'; he would bring out her oddities and mannerisms; her buttons and wrinkles; her ribbons and warts. Her personality would dominate the book. A French writer would rub out all that; he would sacrifice the individual Mrs. Brown to give a more general view of human nature; to make a more abstract, proportioned, and harmonious whole. The Russian would pierce through the flesh; would reveal the soul—the soul alone, wandering out into the Waterloo Road, asking of life some tremendous question which would sound on and on in our ears after the book was finished. And then besides age and country there is the writer's temperament to be considered. You see one thing in character, and I another. You say it means this, and I that. And when it comes to writing, each makes a further selection on principles of his own. Thus Mrs. Brown can be treated in an infinite variety of ways, according to the age, country, and temperament of the writer.

But now I must recall what Mr. Arnold Bennett says. He says that it is only if the characters are real that the novel has any chance of surviving. Otherwise, die it must. But, I ask myself, what is reality? And who are the judges of reality? A character may be real to

Mr. Bennett and quite unreal to me. For instance, in this article he says that Dr. Watson in *Sherlock Holmes*[5] is real to him: to me Dr. Watson is a sack stuffed with straw, a dummy, a figure of fun. And so it is with character after character–in book after book. There is nothing that people differ about more than the reality of characters, especially in contemporary books. But if you take a larger view I think that Mr. Bennett is perfectly right. If, that is, you think of the novels which seem to you great novels–*War and Peace, Vanity Fair, Tristram Shandy, Madame Bovary, Pride and Prejudice, The Mayor of Casterbridge, Villette*–if you think of these books, you do at once think of some character who seemed to you so real (I do not by that mean so lifelike) that it has the power to make you think not merely of it itself, but of all sorts of things through its eyes–of religion, of love, of war, of peace, of family life, of balls in country towns, of sunsets, moonrises, the immortality of the soul. There is hardly any subject of human experience that is left out of *War and Peace* it seems to me. And in all these novels all these great novelists have brought us to see whatever they wish us to see through some character. Otherwise, they would not be novelists; but poets, historians, or pamphleteers.

But now let us examine what Mr. Bennett went on to say–he said that there was no great novelist among the Georgian writers because they cannot create characters who are real, true, and convincing. And there I cannot agree. There are reasons, excuses, possibilities which I think put a different colour upon the case. It seems so to me at least, but I am well aware that this is a matter about which I am likely to be prejudiced, sanguine, and near-sighted. I will put in my view before you in the hope that you will make it impartial, judicial, and broad-minded. Why, then, is it so hard for novelists at present to create characters which seem real, not only to Mr. Bennett, but to the world at large? Why, when October comes round, do the publishers always fail to supply us with a masterpiece?

Surely one reason is that the men and women who began writing novels in 1910 or thereabouts had this great difficulty to face–that there was no English novelist living from whom they could learn their business. Mr. Conrad is a Pole; which sets him apart, and makes him, however admirable, not very helpful. Mr. Hardy has written no novel since 1895. The most prominent and successful novelists in the year 1910 were, I suppose, Mr. Wells, Mr. Bennett, and Mr. Galsworthy. Now it seems to me that to go to these men and ask them to teach you how to write a novel–how to create characters that are real–is precisely like going to a bootmaker and asking him to teach you how to make a watch. Do not let me give you the impression that I do not admire and enjoy their books. They seem to me of great value, and indeed of great necessity. There are seasons when it is more important to have boots than to have watches. To drop metaphor, I think that after the creative activity of the Victorian age it was quite necessary, not only for literature but for life, that someone should write the books that Mr. Wells, Mr. Bennett, and Mr. Galsworthy have written. Yet what odd books they are! Sometimes I wonder if we are right to call them books at all. For they leave one with so strange a feeling of incompleteness and dissatisfaction. In order to complete them it seems necessary to do something–to join a society, or, more desparately, to write a cheque. That done, the restlessness is laid, the book finished; it can be put upon the shelf, and need never be read again. But with the work of other novelists it is different. *Tristram Shandy* or *Pride and Prejudice* is complete in itself; it is self-contained; it leaves one with no desire to do anything, except indeed to read the book again, and to understand it better. The difference perhaps is that both Sterne and Jane Austen were interested in things in themselves; in character in itself; in the book in itself. Therefore everything was inside the book, nothing outside. But the Edwardians were never interested in character in itself; or in the book in itself. They were interested in something outside. Their books, then, were incomplete as books, and required that the reader should finish them, actively and practically, for himself.

Perhaps we can make this clearer if we take the liberty of imagining a little party in the railway carriage–Mr. Wells, Mr. Galsworthy, Mr. Bennett are travelling to Waterloo with Mrs. Brown. Mrs. Brown, I have said, was poorly dressed and very small. She had an anxious, harassed look. I doubt whether she was what you call an educated woman. Seizing upon all these symptoms of the unsatisfactory condition of our primary schools with a rapidity to which I can do no justice, Mr. Wells would instantly project upon the window-pane a vision of a better, breezier, jollier, happier, more adventurous and gallant world, where these musty railway carriages and fusty old women do not exist; where miraculous barges bring tropical fruit to Camberwell by eight o'clock in the morning; where there are public nurseries, fountains, and libraries, dining-rooms, drawing-rooms, and marriages; where every citizen is generous and candid, manly and magnificent, and rather like Mr. Wells himself. But nobody is in the least like Mrs. Brown. There are no Mrs. Browns in Utopia. Indeed I do not think that Mr. Wells, in his passion to make her what she ought to be, would waste a thought upon her as she is. And what would Mr. Galsworthy see? Can we doubt that the walls of Doulton's factory would take his fancy? There are women in that factory who make twenty-five dozen earthenware pots every day. There are mothers in the Mile End Road who depend upon the farthings which those women earn. But there are employers in Surrey who are even now smoking rich cigars while the nightingale sings. Burning with indignation, stuffed with information, arraigning civilisation, Mr. Galsworthy would only see in Mrs. Brown a pot broken on the wheel and thrown into the corner.

Mr. Bennett, alone of the Edwardians, would keep his eyes in the carriage. He, indeed, would observe every detail with immense care. He would notice the advertisements; the pictures of Swanage and Portsmouth; the way in which the cushion bulged between the buttons; how Mrs. Brown wore a brooch which had cost three-and-ten-three at Whitworth's bazaar; and had mended both gloves–indeed the thumb of the left-hand glove had been replaced. And he would observe, at length, how this was the non-stop train from Windsor which calls at Richmond for the convenience of middle-class residents, who can afford to go to the theatre but have not reached the social rank which can afford motor-cars, though it is true, there are occasions (he would tell us what), when they hire them from a company (he would tell us which). And so he would gradually sidle sedately towards Mrs. Brown, and would remark how she had been left a little copyhold, not freehold, property at Datchet, which, however, was mortgaged to Mr. Bungay the solicitor–but why should I presume to invent Mr. Bennett? Does not Mr. Bennett write novels himself? I will open the first book that chance puts in my way–*Hilda Lessways*.[6] Let us see how he makes us feel that Hilda is real, true, and convincing, as a novelist should. She shut the door in a soft, controlled way, which showed the constraint of her relations with her mother. She was fond of reading *Maud*; she was endowed with the power to feel intensely. So far, so good; in his leisurely, surefooted way Mr. Bennett is trying in these first pages, where every touch is important, to show us the kind of girl she was.

But then he begins to describe, not Hilda Lessways, but the view from her bedroom window, the excuse being that Mr. Skellorn, the man who collects rents, is coming along that way. Mr. Bennett proceeds:

'The bailiwick of Turnhill lay behind her; and all the murky district of the Five Towns, of which Turnhill is the northern outpost, lay to the south. At the foot of Chatterley Wood the canal wound in large curves on its way towards the undefiled plains of Cheshire and the sea. On the canal-side, exactly opposite to Hilda's window, was a flour-mill, that

sometimes made nearly as much smoke as the kilns and chimneys
closing the prospect on either hand. From the flour-mill a bricked
path, which separated a considerable row of new cottages from their
appurtenant gardens, led straight into Lessways Street, in front of
Mrs. Lessways' house. By this path Mr. Skellorn should have arrived,
for he inhabited the farthest of the cottages.'

One line of insight would have done more than all those lines of
description; but let them pass as the necessary drudgery of the
novelist. And now–where is Hilda? Alas. Hilda is still looking out of
the window. Passionate and dissatisfied as she was, she was a girl with
an eye for houses. She often compared this old Mr. Skellorn with the
villas she saw from her bedroom window. Therefore the villas must be
described. Mr. Bennett proceeds:

'The row was called Freehold Villas: a consciously proud name in a
district where much of the land was copyhold and could only change
owners subject to the payment of "fines", and to the feudal consent of a
"court" presided over by the agent of a lord of the manor. Most of the
dwellings were owned by their occupiers, who, each an absolute
monarch of the soil, niggled in his sooty garden of an evening amid the
flutter of drying shirts and towels. Freehold Villas symbolized the final
triumph of Victorian economics, the apotheosis of the prudent and
industrious artisan. It corresponded with a Building Society
Secretary's dream of paradise. And indeed it was a very real
achievement. Nevertheless, Hilda's irrational contempt would not
admit this.'

Heaven be praised, we cry! At last we are coming to Hilda herself.
But not so fast. Hilda may have been this, that, and the other; but
Hilda not only looked at houses, and thought of houses; Hilda lived in
a house. And what sort of a house did Hilda live in? Mr. Bennett
proceeds:

'It was one of the two middle houses of a detached terrace of four
houses built by her grandfather Lessways, the teapot manufacturer; it
was the chief of the four, obviously the habitation of the proprietor of
the terrace. One of the corner houses comprised a grocer's shop, and
this house had been robbed of its just proportion of garden so that the
seigneurial garden-plot might be triflingly larger than the other. The
terrace was not a terrace of cottages, but of houses rated at from
twenty-six to thirty-six pounds a year; beyond the means of artisans
and petty insurance agents and rent-collectors. And further, it was
well-built, generously built; and its architecture, though debased,
showed some faint traces of Georgian amenity. It was admittedly the
best row of houses in that newly-settled quarter of the town. In

coming to it out of Freehold Villas Mr. Skellorn obviously came to something superior, wider, more liberal. Suddenly Hilda heard her mother's voice....'

But we cannot hear her mother's voice, or Hilda's voice; we can only hear Mr. Bennett's voice telling us facts about rents and freeholds and copyholds and fines. What can Mr. Bennett be about? I have formed my own opinion of what Mr. Bennett is about–he is trying to make us imagine for him; he is trying to hypnotize us into the belief that, because he has made a house, there must be a person living there. With all his powers of observation, which are marvellous, with all his sympathy and humanity, which are great, Mr. Bennett has never once looked at Mrs. Brown in her corner. There she sits in the corner of the carriage–that carriage which is travelling, not from Richmond to Waterloo, but from one age of English literature to the next, for Mrs. Brown is eternal, Mrs. Brown is human nature, Mrs. Brown changes only on the surface, it is the novelists who get in and out–there she sits and not one of the Edwardian writers has so much as looked at her. They have looked very powerfully, searchingly, and sympathetically out of the window; at factories, at Utopias, even at the decoration and upholstery of the carriage; but never at her, never at life, never at human nature. And so they have developed a technique of novel-writing which suits their purpose; they have made tools and established conventions which do their business. But those tools are not our tools, and that business is not our business. For us those conventions are ruin, those tools are death.

You may well complain of the vagueness of my language. What is a convention, a tool, you may ask, and what do you mean by saying that Mr. Bennett's and Mr. Wells's and Mr. Galsworthy's conventions are the wrong conventions for the Georgians? The question is difficult: I will attempt a short-cut. A convention in writing is not much different from a convention in manners. Both in life and in literature it is necessary to have some means of bridging the gulf between the hostess and her unknown guest on the one hand, the writer and his unknown reader on the other. The hostess bethinks her of the weather, for generations of hostesses have established the fact that this is a subject of universal interest in which we all believe. She begins by saying that we are having a wretched May, and, having thus got into touch with her unknown guest, proceeds to matters of greater interest. So it is in literature. The writer must get into touch with his reader by putting before him something which he recognizes, which therefore stimulates his imagination, and makes him willing to cooperate in the far more difficult business of intimacy. And it is of the highest importance that this common meeting-place should be reached easily, almost instinctively, in the dark, with one's eyes shut. Here is Mr. Bennett making use of this common ground in the passage which I have quoted. The problem before him was to make us believe in the reality of Hilda Lessways. So he began, being an Edwardian, by describing accurately and minutely the sort of house Hilda lived in, and the sort of house she saw from the window. House property was the common ground from which the Edwardians found it easy to proceed to intimacy. Indirect as it seems to us, the convention worked admirably, and thousands of Hilda Lessways were launched upon the world by this means. For that age and generation, the convention was a good one.

But now, if you will allow me to pull my own anecdote to pieces, you will see how keenly I felt the lack of a convention, and how serious a matter it is when the tools of one generation are useless for the next. The incident had made a great impression on me. But how was I to transmit it to you? All I could do was to report as accurately as I could what was said, to describe in detail what was worn, to say, desparingly, that all sorts of scenes rushed into my mind, to proceed to tumble them out pell-mell, and to describe this vivid, this overmastering impression by likening it to a draught or a smell of burning. To tell you the truth, I was also strongly tempted to manufacture a three-volume novel about the old lady's son, and his adventures crossing the Atlantic, and her daughter, and how she kept a milliner's shop in Westminster, the past life of Smith himself, and his house at Sheffield, though such stories seem to me the most dreary, irrelevant, and humbugging affairs in the world.

But if I had done that I should have escaped the appalling effort of saying what I meant. And to have got at what I meant I should have had to go back and back; to experiment with one thing and another; to try this sentence and that, referring each word to my vision, matching it as exactly as possible, and knowing that somehow I had to find a common ground between us, a convention which would not seem to you too odd, unreal, and far-fetched to believe in. I admit that I shirked that arduous undertaking. I let my Mrs. Brown slip through my fingers. I have told you nothing whatever about her. But that is partly the great Edwardians' fault. I asked them—they are my elders and betters—How shall I begin to describe this woman's character? And they said: 'Begin by saying that her father kept a shop in Harrogate. Ascertain the rent. Ascertain the wages of shop assistants in the year 1878. Discover what her mother died of. Describe cancer. Describe calico. Describe—' But I cried: 'Stop! Stop!' And I regret to say that I threw that ugly, that clumsy, that incongruous tool out of the window, for I knew that if I began describing the cancer and the calico, my Mrs. Brown, that vision to which I cling though I know no way of imparting it to you, would have been dulled and tarnished and vanished for ever.

That is what I mean by saying that the Edwardian tools are the wrong ones for us to use. They have laid an enormous stress upon the fabric of things. They have given us a house in the hope that we may be able to deduce the human beings who live there. To give them their due, they have made that house much better worth living in. But if you hold that novels are in the first place about people, and only in the second about the houses they live in, that is the wrong way to set about it. Therefore, you see, the Georgian writer had to begin by throwing away the method that was in use at the moment. He was left alone there facing Mrs. Brown without any method of conveying her to the reader. But that is inaccurate. A writer is never alone. There is always the public with him—if not on the same seat, at least in the compartment next door. Now the public is a strange travelling companion. In England it is a very suggestible and docile creature, which, once you get it to attend, will believe implicitly what it is told for a certain number of years. If you say to the public with sufficient conviction: 'All women have tails, and all men humps,' it will actually learn to see women with tails and men with humps, and will think it very revolutionary and probably improper if you say: 'Nonsense. Monkeys have tails and camels humps. But men and women have brains, and they have hearts; they think and they feel,'—that will seem to it a bad joke, and an improper one into the bargain.

But to return. Here is the British public sitting by the writer's side and saying in its vast and unanimous way: 'Old women have houses. They have fathers. They have incomes. They have servants. They have hot-water bottles. That is how we know that they are old women. Mr. Wells and Mr. Bennett and Mr. Galsworthy have always taught us that this is the way to recognize them. But now with your Mrs. Brown—how are we to believe in her? We do not even know whether her villa was called Albert or Balmoral; what she paid for her gloves; or whether her mother died of cancer or of consumption. How can she be alive? No; she is a mere figment of your imagination.'

And old women of course ought to be made of freehold villas and copyhold estates, not of imagination.

The Georgian novelist, therefore, was in an awkward predicament. There was Mrs. Brown protesting that she was different, quite different, from what people made out, and luring the novelist to her rescue by the most fascinating if fleeting glimpse of her charms; there were the Edwardians handing out tools appropriate to house building and house breaking; and there was the British public asseverating that they must see the hot-water bottle first. Meanwhile the train was rushing to the station where we must all get out.

Such, I think, was the predicament in which the young Georgians found themselves about the year 1910. Many of them—I am thinking of Mr. Forster and Mr. Lawrence in particular—spoilt their early work because, instead of throwing away those tools, they tried to use them. They tried to compromise. They tried to combine their own direct sense of the oddity and significance of some character with Mr. Galsworthy's knowledge of the Factory Acts, and Mr. Bennett's knowledge of the Five Towns. They tried it, but they had too keen, too overpowering a sense of Mrs. Brown and her peculiarities to go on trying it much longer. Something had to be done. At whatever cost to life, limb, and damage to valuable property Mrs. Brown must be rescued, expressed, and set in her high relations to the world before the train stopped and she disappeared for ever. And so the smashing and the crashing began. Thus it is that we hear all round us, in poems and novels and biographies, even in newspaper articles and essays, the sound of breaking and falling, crashing and destruction. It is the prevailing sound of the Georgian age—rather a melancholy one if you think what melodious days there have been in the past, if you think of Shakespeare and Milton and Keats or even of Jane Austen and Thackeray and Dickens; if you think of the language, and the heights to which it can soar when free, and see the same eagle captive, bald, and croaking.

In view of these facts—with these sounds in my ears and these fancies in my brain—I am not going to deny that Mr. Bennett has some reason when he complains that our Georgian writers are unable to make us believe that our characters are real. I am forced to agree that they do not pour out three immortal masterpieces with Victorian regularity every autumn. But, instead of being gloomy, I am sanguine. For this state of things is, I think, inevitable whenever from hoar old age or callow youth the convention ceases to be a means of communication between writer and reader, and becomes instead an obstacle and an impediment. At the present moment we are suffering, not from decay, but from having no code of manners which writers and readers accept as a prelude to the more exciting intercourse of friendship. The literary convention of the time is so artificial—you have to talk about the weather and nothing but the weather throughout the entire visit—that, naturally, the feeble are tempted to outrage, and the strong are led to destroy the very foundations and rules of literary society. Signs of this are everywhere apparent. Grammar is violated; syntax disintegrated; as a boy staying with an aunt for the week-end rolls in the geranium bed out of sheer desperation as the solemnities of the sabbath wear on. The more adult writers do not, of course, indulge in wuch wanton exhibitions of spleen. Their sincerity is desperate, and their courage tremendous; it is only that they do not know which to use, a fork or their fingers. Thus, if you read Mr. Joyce and Mr. Eliot you will be struck by the indecency of the one, and the obscurity of the other. Mr. Joyce's indecency in *Ulysses* seems to me the conscious and calculated indecency of a desperate man who feels that in order to breathe he must break the windows. At moments, when the window is broken, he is magnificent. But what a waste of energy! And, after all, how dull indecency is, when it is not the overflowing of a superabundant energy or savagery, but the determined and public-spirited act of a man who needs fresh air! Again, with the obscurity of Mr. Eliot. I think that Mr. Eliot has written some of the loveliest single lines in modern poetry. But how intolerant he is of the old usages and politenesses of society–respect for the weak, consideration for the dull! As I sun myself upon the intense and ravishing beauty of one of his lines, and reflect that I must make a dizzy and dangerous leap to the next, and so on from line to line, like an acrobat flying precariously from bar to bar, I cry out, I confess, for the old decorums, and envy the indolence of my ancestors who, instead of spinning madly through mid-air, dreamt quietly in the shade with a book. Again, in Mr. Strachey's books, *Eminent Victorians* and *Queen Victoria*,[7] the effort and strain of writing against the grain and current of the times is visible too. It is much less visible, of course, for not only is he dealing with facts, which are stubborn things, but he has fabricated, chiefly from eighteenth-century material, a very discreet code of manners of his own, which allows him to sit at the table with the highest in the land and to say a great many things under cover of that exquisite apparel which, had they gone naked, would have been chased by the men-servants from the room. Still, if you compare *Eminent Victorians* with some of Lord Macaulay's[8] essays, though you will feel that Lord Macaulay is always wrong, and Mr. Strachey always right, you will also feel a body, a sweep, a richness in Lord Macaulay's essays which show that his age was behind him; all his strength went straight into his work; none was used for purposes of concealment or of conversion. But Mr. Strachey has had to open our eyes before he made us see; he has had to search out and sew together a very artful manner of speech; and the effort, beautifully though it is concealed, has robbed his work of some of the force that should have gone into it, and limited his scope.

For these reasons, then, we must reconcile ourselves to a season of failures and fragments. We must reflect that where so much strength is spent on finding a way of telling the truth, the truth itself is bound to reach us in rather an exhausted and chaotic condition. Ulysses, Queen Victoria, Mr. Prufrock—to give Mrs. Brown some of the names she has made famous lately—is a little pale and dishevelled by the time her rescuers reach her. And it is the sound of their axes that we hear—a vigorous and stimulating sound in my ears—unless of course you wish to sleep, when, in the bounty of his concern, Providence has provided a host of writers anxious and able to satisfy your needs.

Thus I have tried, at tedious length, I fear, to answer some of the questions which I began by asking. I have given an account of some of the difficulties which in my view beset the Georgian writer in all his forms. I have sought to excuse him. May I end by venturing to remind you of the duties and responsibilities that are yours as partners in this business of writing books, as companions in the railway carriage, as fellow travellers with Mrs. Brown? For she is just as visible to you who remain silent as to us who tell stories about her. In the course of your daily life this past week you have had far stranger and more interesting experiences than the one I have tried to describe. You have overheard scraps of talk that filled you with amazement. You have gone to bed at night bewildered by the complexity of your feelings. In one day thousands of ideas have coursed through your brains; thousands of emotions have met, collided, and disappeared in astonishing disorder. Nevertheless, you allow the writers to palm off upon you a version of all this, an image of Mrs. Brown, which has no likeness to that surprising apparition whatsoever. In your modesty you seem to consider that writers are of different blood and bone from yourselves; that they know more of Mrs. Brown than you do. Never was there a more fatal mistake. It is this division between reader and writer, this humility on your part, these professional airs and graces on ours, that corrupt and emasculate the books which should be the healthy offspring of a close and equal alliance between us. Hence spring those sleek, smooth novels, those portentous and ridiculous biographies, that milk and watery criticism, those poems melodiously celebrating the innocence of roses and sheep which pass so plausibly for literature at the present time.

Your part is to insist that writers shall come down off their plinths and pedestals, and describe beautifully if possible, truthfully at any rate, our Mrs. Brown. You should insist that she is an old lady of unlimited capacity and infinite variety; capable of appearing in any place, wearing any dress; saying anything and doing heaven knows what. But the things she says and the things she does and her eyes and her nose and her speech and her silence have an overwhelming fascination, for she is, of course, the spirit we live by, life itself.

But do not expect just at present a complete and satisfactory presentment of her. Tolerate the spasmodic, the obscure, the fragmentary, the failure. Your help is invoked in a good cause. For I will make one final and surpassingly rash prediction–we are trembling on the verge of one of the great ages of English literature. But it can only be reached if we are determined never, never to desert Mrs. Brown.

1 Bennett's article, 'Is the Novel Decaying?', appeared in *Cassell's Weekly*, 28 March 1923. It is included in *Virginia Woolf: The Critical Heritage* ed. R. Majumdar and A. McLaurin (1975).
2 Butler (1835-1902) wrote *The Way of All Flesh* as a criticism of the Victorian way of life, but it was not published until 1903, after his death.
3 The daily paper supporting the Labour Party.
4 Jane Carlyle (1801-66) was a remarkable woman, whose talents were sacrificed to the service of hur husband Thomas (1795-1881), the social critic and moralist.
5 Sir Arthur Conan Doyle (1859-1930) created the famous detective and his companion in *The Adventures of Sherlock Holmes* in 1891.
6 One of the Clayhanger series, published in 1911; the quotations come from Ch. I, Section 3.
7 Lytton Strachey (1880-1932) published *Eminent Victorians* in 1918 and *Queen Victoria* in 1921.
8 Thomas Babington Macaulay (1800-59), the Victorian essayist and historian.

D. H. Lawrence

David Herbert Lawrence (1885-1930) had his first poems published by Ford in The English Review. *His novels included* Sons and Lovers *(1913),* The Rainbow *(1915),* Women in Love *(1920),* Aaron's Rod *(1922) and* Lady Chatterley's Lover *(1928); volumes of poetry were* Love Poems and Others *(1913),* Amores *(1916),* Look We Have Come Through *(1917),* New Poems *(1918), and* Birds, Beasts and Flowers *(1923). His critical book* Studies in Classic American Literature *appeared in 1923.*

An excellent selection of his criticism was edited by Anthony Beal in 1956 as D.H. Lawrence. Selected Literary Criticism. *There is now a scholarly edition of* A Study of Thomas Hardy and Other Essays *(1985), edited by Brian Steele.*

18 Preface to New Poems, 1920

New Poems *was published in London in 1918; the American edition of 1920 included a 'Preface', which had first appeared in* Playboy *Nos. 4 and 5 (1919) as 'Poetry of the Present', and in* Voices *(October 1919) as 'Verse Free and Unfree'.*

It seems when we hear a skylark singing as if sound were running into the future, running so fast and utterly without consideration, straight on into futurity. And when we hear a nightingale, we hear the pause and the rich, piercing rhythm of recollection, the perfected past. The lark may sound sad, but with the lovely lapsing sadness that is almost a swoon of hope. The nightingale's triumph is a pæan, but a death-pæan.

So it is with poetry. Poetry is, as a rule, either the voice of the far future, exquisite and ethereal, or it is the voice of the past, rich, magnificent. When the Greeks heard the *Iliad* and the *Odyssey*, they heard their own past calling in their hearts, as men far inland sometimes hear the sea and fall weak with powerful, wonderful regret, nostalgia; or else their own future rippled its time-beats through their blood, as they followed the painful, glamorous progress of the

Ithacan.[1] This was Homer to the Greeks: their Past, splendid with battles won and death achieved, and their Future, the magic wandering of Ulysses through the unknown.

With us it is the same. Our birds sing on the horizons. They sing out of the blue, beyond us, or out of the quenched night. They sing at dawn and sunset. Only the poor, shrill, tame canaries whistle while we talk. The wild birds begin before we are awake, or as we drop into dimness, out of waking. Our poets sit by the gateways, some by the east, some by the west. As we arrive and as we go out our hearts surge with response. But whilst we are in the midst of life, we do not hear them.

The poetry of the beginning and the poetry of the end must have that exquisite finality, perfection which belongs to all that is far off. It is in the realm of all that is perfect. It is of the nature of all that is complete and consummate. This completeness, this consummateness, the finality and the perfection are conveyed in exquisite form: the perfect symmetry, the rhythm which returns upon itself like a dance where the hands link and loosen and link for the supreme moment of the end. Perfected bygone moments, perfected moments in the glimmering futurity, these are the treasured gem-like lyrics of Shelley and Keats.

But there is another kind of poetry: the poetry of that which is at hand: the immediate present. In the immediate present there is no perfection, no consummation, nothing finished. The strands are all flying, quivering, intermingling into the web, the waters are shaking the moon. There is no round, consummate moon on the face of running water, nor on the face of the unfinished tide. There are no gems of the living plasm. The living plasm vibrates unspeakably, it inhales the future, it exhales the past, it is the quick of both, and yet it is neither. There is no plasmic finality, nothing crystal, permanent. If we try to fix the living tissue, as the biologists fix it with formation, we have only a hardened bit of the past, the bygone life under our observation.

Life, the ever-present, knows no finality, no finished crystallisation. The perfect rose is only a running flame, emerging and flowing off, and never in any sense at rest, static, finished. Herein lies its transcendent loveliness. The whole tide of all life and all time suddenly heaves, and appears before us as an apparition, a revelation. We look at the very white quick of nascent creation. A water-lily heaves herself from the flood, looks around, gleams, and is gone. We have seen the incarnation, the quick of the ever-swirling flood. We have seen the invisible. We have seen, we have touched, we have partaken of the very substance of creative change, creative mutation. If you tell me about the lotus, tell me of nothing changeless or eternal. Tell me of the mystery of the inexhaustible, forever-unfolding creative spark. Tell me of the incarnate disclosure of the flux, mutation in blossom, laughter and decay perfectly open in their transit, nude in their movement before us.

Let me feel the mud and the heavens in my lotus. Let me feel the heavy, silting, sucking mud, the spinning of sky winds. Let me feel them both in purest contact, the nakedness of sucking weight, nakedly passing radiance. Give me nothing fixed, set, static. Don't give me the infinite or the eternal: nothing of infinity, nothing of eternity. Give me the still, white seething, the incandescence and the coldness of the incarnate moment: the moment, the quick of all change and haste and opposition: the moment, the immediate present, the Now. The immediate moment is not a drop of water running downstream. It is the source and issue, the bubbling up of the stream. Here, in this very instant moment, up bubbles the stream of time, out of the wells of futurity, flowing on to the oceans of the past. The source, the issue, the creative quick.

There is poetry of this immediate present, instant poetry, as well as poetry of the infinite past and the infinite future. The seething poetry of the incarnate Now is supreme, beyond even the everlasting gems of the before and after. In its quivering momentaneity is surpasses the crystalline, pearl-hard jewels, the poems of the eternities. Do not ask for the qualities of the unfading timeless gems. Ask for the whiteness which is the seethe of mud, ask for that incipient putrescence which is the skies falling, ask for the never-pausing, never-ceasing life itself. There must be mutation, swifter than iridescence, haste, not rest, come-and-go, not fixity, inconclusiveness, immediacy, the quality of life itself, without denouement or close. There must be the rapid momentaneous association of things which meet and pass on the for ever incalculable journey of creation: everything left in its own rapid, fluid relationship with the rest of things.

This is the unrestful, ungraspable poetry of the sheer present, poetry whose very permanency lies in its wind-like transit. Whitman's[2] is the best poetry of this kind. Without beginning and without end, without any base and pediment, it sweeps past for ever, like a wind that is for ever in passage, and unchainable. Whitman truly looked before and after. But he did not sigh for what is not. The clue to all his utterance lies in the sheer appreciation of the instant moment, life surging itself into utterance at its very well-head. Eternity is only an abstraction from the actual present. Infinity is only a great reservoir of recollection, or a reservoir of aspiration: man-made. The quivering nimble hour of the present, this is the quick of Time. This is the immanence. The quick of the universe is the *pulsating, carnal self*, mysterious and palpable. So it is always.

Because Whitman put this into his poetry, we fear him and respect him so profoundly. We should not fear him if he sang only of the 'old unhappy far-off things',[3] or of the 'wings of the morning'.[4] It is because his heart beats with the urgent, insurgent Now, which is even upon us all, that we dread him. He is so near the quick.

From the foregoing it is obvious that the poetry of the instant present cannot have the same body or the same motion as the poetry of the before and after. It can never submit to the same conditions. It is never finished. There is no rhythm which returns upon itself, no serpent of eternity with its tail in its own mouth. There is no static perfection, none of that finality which we find so satisfying because we are so frightened.

Much has been written about free verse. But all that can be said, first and last, is that free verse is, or should be, direct utterance from the instant, whole man. It is the soul and the mind and body surging at once, nothing left out. They speak all together. There is some confusion, some discord. But the confusion and the discord only belong to the reality, as noise belongs to the plunge of water. It is no use inventing fancy laws for free verse, no use drawing a melodic line which all the feet must toe. Free verse toes no melodic line, no matter what drill-sergeant. Whitman pruned away his clichés–perhaps his clichés of rhythm as well as of phrase. And this is about all we can do, deliberately, with free verse. We can get rid of the stereotyped movements and the old hackneyed associations of sound or sense. We can break down those artificial conduits and canals through which we do so love to force our utterance. We can break the stiff neck of habit. We can be in ourselves spontaneous and flexible as flame, we can see that utterance rushes out without artificial form or artificial smoothness. But we cannot positively prescribe any motion, any rhythm. All the laws we invent or discover–it amounts to pretty much the same–will fail to apply to free verse. They will only apply to some form of restricted, limited unfree verse.

All we can say is that free verse does *not* have the same nature as restricted verse. It is not of the nature of reminiscence. It is not the past which we treasure in its perfection between our hands. Neither is it the crystal of the perfect future, into which we gaze. Its tide is neither the full, yearning flow of aspiration, nor the sweet, poignant ebb of remembrance and regret. The past and the future are the two great bournes of human emotion, the two great homes of the human days, the two eternities. They are both conclusive, final. Their beauty is the beauty of the goal, finished, perfected. Finished beauty and measured symmetry belong to the stable, unchanging eternities.

But in free verse we look for the insurgent naked throb of the instant moment. To break the lovely form of metrical verse, and to dish up the fragments as a new substance, called *vers libre*, this is what most of the free-versifiers accomplish. They do not know that free verse has its own *nature*, that it is neither star nor pearl, but instantaneous like plasm. It has no goal in either eternity. It has no finish. It has no satisfying stability, satisfying to those who like the immutable. None of this. It is the instant; the quick; the very jetting source of all will-be and has-been. The utterance is like a spasm, naked contact with all influences at once. It does not want to get anywhere. It just takes place.

For such utterance any externally applied law would be mere shackles and death. The law must come new each time from within. The bird is on the wing in the winds, flexible to every breath, a living spark in the storm, its very flickering depending upon its supreme mutability and power of change. Whence such a bird came: whither it goes: from what solid earth it rose up, and upon what solid earth it will close its wings and settle, this is not the question. This is a question of before and after. Now, *now*, the bird is on the wing in the winds.

Such is the rare new poetry. One realm we have never conquered: the pure present. One great mystery of time is *terra incognita* to us: the instant. The most superb mystery we have hardly recognised: the immediate, instant self. The quick of all time is the instant. The quick of all the universe, of all creation, is the incarnate, carnal self. Poetry gave us the clue: free verse: Whitman. Now we know.

The ideal—what is the ideal? A figment. An abstraction. A static abstraction, abstracted from life. It is a fragment of the before or the after. It is a crystallised aspiration, or a crystallised remembrance: crystallised, set, finished. It is a thing set apart, in the great storehouse of eternity, the storehouse of finished things.

We do not speak of things crystallised and set apart. We speak of the instant, the immediate self, the very plasm of the self. We speak also of free verse.

All this should have come as a preface to *Look! We Have Come Through!* But is it not better to publish a preface long after the book it belongs to has appeared? For then the reader will have had his fair chance with the book, alone.

1   Ulysses (Odysseus) was the King of Ithaca.
2   Walt Whitman (1819-92), the American poet who wrote *Leaves of Grass* (1855-60) in
     free verse.
3   From Wordsworth's 'The Solitary Reaper' (1803).
4   From the opening of *Psalm CXXXIX*.

19 'Surgery for the Novel– or a Bomb?', 1923

First published in the Readers' Digest International Book Review *for April 1923.*

You talk about the future of the baby, little cherub, when he's in the cradle cooing; and it's a romantic, glamorous subject. You also talk, with the parson, about the future of the wicked old grandfather who is at last lying on his death-bed. And there again you have a subject for much vague emotion, chiefly of fear this time.

How do we feel about the novel? Do we bounce with joy thinking of the wonderful novelistic days ahead? Or do we grimly shake our heads and hope the wicked creatue will be spared a little longer? Is the novel on his death-bed, old sinner? Or is he just toddling round his cradle, sweet little thing? Let us have another look at him before we decide this rather serious case.

There he is, the monster with many faces, many branches to him, like a tree: the modern novel. And he is almost dual, like Siamese twins. On the one hand, the pale-faced, high-browed, earnest novel, which you have to take seriously; on the other, that smirking, rather plausible hussy, the popular novel.

Let us just for the moment feel the pulses of *Ulysses* and of Miss Dorothy Richardson[1] and M. Marcel Proust,[2] on the earnest side of Briareus,[3] on the other, the throb of *The Sheik*[4] and Mr. Zane Grey,[5] and, if you will, Mr. Robert Chambers[6] and the rest. Is *Ulysses* in his cradle? Oh, dear! What a grey face! And *Pointed Roofs*, are they a gay little toy for nice little girls? And M. Proust? Alas! You can hear the death-rattle in their throats. They can hear it themselves. They are listening to it with acute interest, trying to discover whether the intervals are minor thirds or major fourths. Which is rather infantile, really.

So there you have the 'serious' novel, dying in a very long-drawn-out fourteen-volume death-agony, and absorbedly, childishly interested in the phenomenon. 'Did I feel a twinge in my little toe, or didn't I?' asks every character of Mr. Joyce or of Miss Richardson or M. Proust. Is my aura a blend of frankincense and orange pekoe and boot-blacking, or is it myrrh and bacon-fat and Shetland tweed? The audience round the death-bed gapes for the answer. And when, in a sepulchral tone, the answer comes at length, after hundreds of pages: 'It is none of these, it is abysmal chloro-coryambasis,'[7] the audience quivers all over, and murmurs: 'That's just how I feel myself.'

Which is the dismal, long-drawn-out comedy of the death-bed of the serious novel. It is self-consciousness picked into such fine bits that the bits are most of them invisible, and you have to go by smell. Through thousands and thousands of pages Mr. Joyce and Miss Richardson tear themselves to pieces, strip their smallest emotions to the finest threads, till you feel you are sewed inside a mattress that is being slowly shaken up, and you are turning to wool along with the rest of the woolliness.

It's awful. And it's childish. It really is childish, after a certain age, to be absorbedly self-conscious. One has to be self-conscious at seventeen: still a little self-conscious at twenty-seven; but if we are going it strong at thirty-seven, then it is a sign of arrested development, nothing else. And if it is still continuing at forty-seven, it is obvious senile precocity.

And there's the serious novel: senile-precocious. Absorbedly, childishly concerned with *what I am.* 'I am this, I am that, I am the other. My reactions are such, and such, and such. And, oh, Lord, if I liked to watch myself closely enough, if I liked to analyse my feelings minutely, as I unbutton my gloves, instead of saying crudely I unbuttoned them, then I could go on to a million pages instead of a thousand. In fact, the more I come to think of it, it is gross, it is uncivilised bluntly to say: I unbuttoned my gloves. After all, the absorbing adventure of it! Which button did I begin with?' etc.

The people in the serious novels are so absorbedly concerned with themselves and what they feel and don't feel, and how they react to every mortal button; and their audience as frenziedly absorbed in the application of the author's discoveries to their own reactions: 'That's me! That's exactly it! I'm just finding myself in this book!' Why, this is more than death-bed, it is almost post-mortem behaviour.

Some convulsion or cataclysm will have to get this serious novel out of its self-consciousness. The last great war made it worse. What's to be done? Because, poor thing, it's really young yet. The novel has never become fully adult. It has never quite grown to years of discretion. It has always youthfully hoped for the best, and felt rather sorry for itself on the last page. Which is just childish. The childishness has become very long-drawn-out. So very many adolescents who drag their adolescence on into their forties and their fifties and their sixties! There needs some sort of surgical operation, somewhere.

Then the popular novels–the *Sheiks* and *Babbitts*[8] and Zane Grey novels. They are just as self-conscious, only they do have more illusions about themselves. The heroines do think they are lovelier, and more fascinating, and purer. The heroes do see themselves more heroic, braver, more chivalrous, more fetching. The mass of the populace 'find themselves' in the popular novels. But nowadays it's a funny sort of self they find. A sheik with a whip up his sleeve, and a heroine with weals on her back, but adored in the end, adored, the whip out of sight, but the weals still faintly visible.

It's a funny sort of self they discover in the popular novels. And the essential moral of *If Winter Comes*,[9] for example, is so shaky. 'The gooder you are, the worse it is for you, poor you, oh, poor you. Don't you be so blimey good, it's not good enough.' Or *Babbitt:* 'Go on, you make your pile, and then pretend you're too good for it. Put it over the rest of the grabbers that way. They're only pleased with themselves when they've made their pile. You go one better.'

Always the same sort of baking-powder gas to make you rise: the soda counteracting the cream of tartar, and the tartar counteracted by the soda. Sheik heroines, duly whipped, wildly adored. Babbitts with solid fortunes, weeping from self-pity. Winter-Comes heroes as good as pie, hauled off to jail. *Moral:* Don't be too good, because you'll go to jail for it. *Moral:* Don't feel sorry for yourself till you've made your pile and don't need to feel sorry for yourself. *Moral:* Don't let him adore you till he's whipped you into it. Then you'll be partners in mild crime as well as in holy matrimony.

Which again is childish. Adolescence which *can't* grow up. Got into the self-conscious rut and going crazy, quite crazy in it. Carrying on their adolescence into middle age and old age, like the looney Cleopatra[10] in *Dombey and Son*, murmuring 'Rose-coloured curtains' with her dying breath.

The future of the novel? Poor old novel, it's in a rather dirty, messy tight corner. And it's either got to get over the wall or knock a hole through it. In other words, it's got to grow up. Put away childish things like: 'Do I love the girl, or don't I?'–'Am I pure and sweet, or am I not?'–'Do I unbutton my right glove first, or my left?'–'Did my mother ruin my life by refusing to drink the cocoa which my bride had boiled for her?' These questions and their answers don't really interest me any more, though the world still goes sawing them over. I simply don't care for any of these things now, though I used to. The purely emotional and self-analytical stunts are played out in me. I'm finished. I'm deaf to the whole band. But I'm neither *blasé* nor cynical, for all that. I'm just interested in something else.

Supposing a bomb were put under the whole scheme of things, what would we be after? What feelings do we want to carry though into the next epoch? What feelings will carry us through? What is the underlying impulse in us that will provide the motive power for a new state of things, when this democratic-industrial-lovey-dovey-darling-take-me-to-mamma state of things is bust?

What next? That's what interests me. 'What now?' is no fun any more.

If you wish to look into the past for what-next books, you can go back to the Greek philosophers. Plato's Dialogues are queer little novels. It seems to me it was the greatest pity in the world, when philosophy and fiction got split. They used to be one, right from the days of myth. Then they went and parted, like a nagging married couple, with Aristotle and Thomas Aquinas and that beastly Kant.[11] So the novel went sloppy, and philosophy went abstract-dry. The two should come together again – in the novel.

You've got to find a new impulse for new things in mankind, and it's really fatal to find it through abstraction. No, no; philosophy and religion, they've both gone too far on the algebraical tack: Let X stand for sheep and Y for goats: then X minus Y equals Heaven, and X plus Y equals Earth, and Y minus X equals Hell. Thank you! But what coloured shirt does X have on?

The novel has a future. It's got to have the courage to tackle new propositions without using abstractions; it's got to present us with new, really new feelings, a whole line of new emotion, which will get us out of the emotional rut. Instead of snivelling about what is and has been, or inventing new sensations in the old line, it's got to break a way through, like a hole in the wall. And the public will scream and say it is sacrilege: because, of course, when you've been jammed for a long time in a tight corner, and you get really used to its stuffiness and its tightness, till you find it suffocatingly cosy; then, of course, you're horrified when you see a new glaring hole in what was your cosy wall. You're horrified. You back away from the cold stream of fresh air as if it were killing you. But gradually, first one and then another of the sheep filters through the gap and finds a new world outside.

1 Dorothy Richardson (1873-1937) was a pioneer of the stream-of-consciousness method in the novels of her 'Pilgrimage' sequence published between 1915 and 1938; *Pointed Roofs* was the first.

2 Marcel Proust (1871-1922), the French novelist, wrote *A la Recherche du Temps Perdu*, published in eight parts between 1913 and 1927, the last three posthumously.

3 The dividing-line; the Pillars of Briareos was another name for the Pillars of Hercules.
4 A popular romantic novel of 1919 by Edith M. Hull.
5 (1872-1932), a popular novelist, writer of Westerns.
6 (1865-1933), a popular novelist, writer of historical romances.
7 An impressive-sounding but meaningless phrase invented by Lawrence.
8 *Babbitt*, a successful novel by the American novelist, Sinclair Lewis (1885-1951), published in 1922.
9 A popular novel of 1921, by A.S.M. Hutchinson (1879-1971).
10 Mrs Skewton, a comic figure in Dickens's novel *Dombey and Son* (1848).
11 Immanuel Kant (1724-1804), the German Romantic philosopher.

20 'Morality and the Novel', 1925

First published in The Calendar of Modern Letters *II, 10 (December 1925), 269-74.*

The business of art is to reveal the relation between man and his circumambient universe, at the living moment. As mankind is always struggling in the toils of old relationships, art is always ahead of the 'times', which themselves are always far in the rear of the living moment.

When van Gogh paints sunflowers, he reveals, or achieves, the vivid relation between himself, as man, and the sunflower, as sunflower, at that quick moment of time. His painting does not represent the sunflower itself. We shall never know what the sunflower itself is. And the camera will *visualise* the sunflower far more perfectly than van Gogh can.

The vision on the canvas is a third thing, utterly intangible and inexplicable, the offspring of the sunflower itself and van Gogh himself. The vision on the canvas is for ever incommensurable with the canvas, or the paint, or van Gogh as a human organism, or the sunflower as a botanical organism. You cannot weigh nor measure nor even describe the vision on the canvas. It exists, to tell the truth, only in the much-debated fourth dimension. In dimensional space it has no existence.

It is a revelation of the perfected relation, at a certain moment, between a man and a sunflower. It is neither man-in-the-mirror nor flower-in-the-mirror, neither is it above or below or across anything. It is between everything, in the fourth dimension.

And this perfected relation between man and his circumambient universe is life itself, for mankind. It has the fourth-dimensional quality of eternity and perfection. Yet it is momentaneous.

Man and the sunflower both pass away from the moment, in the process of forming a new relationship. The relation between all things changes from day to day, in a subtle stealth of change. Hence art, which reveals or attains to another perfect relationship, will be for ever new.

At the same time, that which exists in the non-dimensional space of pure relationship is deathless, lifeless, and eternal. That is, it gives us the *feeling* of being beyond life or death. We say an Assyrian lion or an Egyptian hawk's head 'lives'. What we really mean is that it is beyond life, and therefore beyond death. It gives us that feeling. And there is something inside us which must also be beyond life and beyond death, since that 'feeling' which we get from an Assyrian lion or an Egyptian hawk's head is so infinitely precious to us. As the evening star, that spark of pure relation between night and day, has been precious to man since time began.

If we think about it, we find that our life *consists in* this achieving of a pure relationship between ourselves and the living universe about us. This is how I 'save my soul' by accomplishing a pure relationship between me and another person, me and other people, me and a nation, me and a race of men, me and the animals, me and the trees or flowers, me and the earth, me and the skies and sun and stars, me and the moon: an infinity of pure relations, big and little, like the stars of the sky: that makes our eternity, for each one of us, me and the timber I am sawing, the lines of force I follow; me and the dough I knead for bread, me and the very motion with which I write, me and the bit of gold I have got. This, if we knew it, is our life and our eternity: the subtle, perfected relation between me and my whole circumambient universe.

And morality is that delicate, for ever trembling and changing *balance* between me and my circumambient universe, which precedes and accompanies a true relatedness.

Now here we see the beauty and the great value of the novel. Philosophy, religion, science, they are all of them busy nailing things down, to get a stable equilibrium. Religion, with its nailed-down One God, who says *Thou shalt, Thou shan't*, and hammers home every time; philosophy, with its fixed ideas; science with its 'laws': they, all of them, all the time, want to nail us on to some tree or other.

But the novel, no. The novel is the highest example of subtle inter-relatedness that man has discovered. Everything is true in its own time, place, circumstance, and untrue outside of its own place, time, circumstance. If you try to nail anything down, in the novel, either it kills the novel, or the novel gets up and walks away with the nail.

Morality in the novel is the trembling instability of the balance. When the novelist puts his thumb in the scale, to pull down the balance to his own predilection, that is immorality.

The modern novel tends to become more and more immoral, as the novelist tends to press his thumb heavier and heavier in the pan: either on the side of love, pure love: or on the side of licentious 'freedom'.

The novel is not, as a rule, immoral because the novelist has any dominant *idea*, or *purpose*. The immorality lies in the novelist's helpless, unconscious predilection. Love is a great emotion. But if you set out to write a novel, and you yourself are in the throes of the great predilection for love, love as the supreme, the only emotion worth living for, then you will write an immoral novel.

Because *no* emotion is supreme, or exclusively worth living for. *All* emotions go to the achieving of a living relationship between a human being and the other human being or creature or thing he becomes purely related to. All emotions, including love and hate, and rage and tenderness, go to the adjusting of the oscillating, unestablished balance between two people who amount to anything. If the novelist puts his thumb in the pan, for love, tenderness, sweetness, peace, then he commits an immoral act: he *prevents* the possibility of a pure relationship, a pure relatedness, the only thing that matters: and he makes inevitable the horrible reaction, when he lets his thumb go, towards hate and brutality, cruelty and destruction.

Life is so made that opposites sway about a trembling centre of balance. The sins of the fathers are visited on the children. If the fathers drag down the balance on the side of love, peace, and production, then in the third or fourth generation the balance will swing back violently to hate, rage, and destruction. We must balance as we go.

And of all the art forms, the novel most of all demands the trembling and oscillating of the balance. The 'sweet' novel is more falsified, and therefore more immoral, than the blood-and-thunder novel.

The same with the smart and smudgily cynical novel, which says it doesn't matter what you do, because one thing is as good as another, anyhow, and prostitution is just as much 'life' as anything else.

This misses the point entirely. A thing isn't life just because somebody does it. This the artist ought to know perfectly well. The ordinary bank clerk buying himself a new straw hat isn't 'life' at all: it is just existence, quite all right, like everyday dinners: but not 'life'.

By life, we mean something that gleams, that has the fourth-dimensional quality. If the bank clerk feels really piquant about his hat, if he establishes a lively relation with it, and goes out of the shop with the new straw on his head, a changed man, be-aureoled, then that is life.

The same with the prostitute. If a man establishes a living relation to her, if only for one moment, then it is life. But if it *doesn't*: if it is just money and function, then it is not life, but sordidness, and a betrayal of living.

If a novel reveals true and vivid relationships, it is a moral work, no matter what the relationships may consist in. If the novelist *honours* the relationship in itself, it will be a great novel.

But there are so many relationships which are not real. When the man in *Crime and Punishment* murders the old woman for sixpence, although it is *actual* enough, it is never quite real. The balance between the murderer and the old woman is gone entirely; it is only a mess. It is actuality, but it is not 'life', in the living sense.

The popular novel, on the other hand, dishes up a *réchauffé* of old relationships: *If Winter Comes.* And old relationships dished up are likewise immoral. Even a magnificent painter like Raphael does nothing more than dress up in gorgeous new dress relationships which have already been experienced. And this gives a gluttonous kind of pleasure of the mass: a voluptuousness, a wallowing. For centuries, men say of their voluptuously ideal woman: 'She is a Raphael Madonna.' And woman are only just learning to take it as an insult.

A new relation, a new relatedness hurts somewhat in the attaining; and will always hurt. So life will always hurt. Because real voluptuousness lies in re-acting old relationships, and at the best, getting an alcoholic sort of pleasure out of it, slightly depraving.

Each time we strive to a new relation, with anyone or anything, it is bound to hurt somewhat. Because it means the struggle with and the displacing of old connexions, and this is never pleasant. And moreover, between living things at least, an adjustment means also a fight, for each party, inevitably, must 'seek its own' in the other, and be denied. When, in the parties, each of them seeks his own, her own, absolutely, then it is a fight to the death. And this is true of the thing called 'passion'. On the other hand, when, of the two parties, one yields utterly to the other, this is called sacrifice, and it also means death. So the Constant Nymph[1] died of her eighteen months of constancy.

It isn't the nature of nymphs to be constant. She should have been constant in her nymph-hood. And it is unmanly to accept sacrifices. He should have abided by his own manhood.

There is, however, the third thing; which is neither sacrifice nor fight to the death: when each seeks only the true relatedness to the other. Each must be true to himself, herself, his own manhood, her own womanhood, and let the relationship work out of itself. This means courage above all things: and then discipline. Courage to accept the life-thrust from within oneself, and from the other person. Discipline, not to exceed oneself any more than one can help. Courage, when one has exceeded oneself, to accept the fact and not whine about it.

Obviously, to read a really new novel will *always* hurt, to some extent. There will always be resistance. The same with new pictures, new music. You may judge of their reality by the fact that they do arouse a certain resistance, and compel, at length, a certain acquiescence.

The great relationship, for humanity, will always be the relation between man and woman. The relation between man and man, woman and woman, parent and child, will always be subsidiary.

And the relation between man and woman will change for ever, and will for ever be the new central clue to human life. It is the *relation itself* which is the quick and the central clue to life, not the man, nor the woman, nor the children that result from the relationship, as a contingency.

It is no use thinking you can put a stamp on the relation between man and woman, to keep it in the *status quo*. You can't. You might as well try to put a stamp on the rainbow or the rain.

As for the bond of love, better put it off when it galls. It is an absurdity, to say that men and women *must love*. Men and women will be for ever subtly and changingly related to one another; no need to yoke them with any 'bond' at all. The only morality is to have man true to his manhood, woman to her womanhood, and let the relationship form of itself, in all honour. For it is, to each, *life itself.*

If we are going to be moral, let us refrain from driving pegs through anything, either through each other or through the third thing, the relationship, which is for ever the ghost of both of us. Every sacrificial crucifixion needs five pegs, four short ones and a long one, each one an abomination. But when you try to nail down the relationship itself, and write over it *Love* instead of *This is the King of the Jews*, then you can go on putting in nails for ever. Even Jesus called it the Holy Ghost, to show you that you can't lay salt on its tail.

The novel is a perfect medium for revealing to us the changing rainbow of our living relationships. The novel can help us to live, as nothing else can: no didactic Scripture, anyhow. If the novelist keeps his thumb out of the pan.

But when the novelist *has* his thumb in the pan, the novel becomes an unparalleled perverter of men and women. To be compared only, perhaps, to that great mischief of sentimental hymns, like 'Lead, Kindly Light,'[2] which have helped to rot the marrow in the bones of the present generation.

1   *The Constant Nymph* (1924) was a popular romantic novel by Margaret Kennedy (1896-1967).
2   The hymn was written by John Henry Newman (1801-90).

21 'Why the Novel Matters', 1925
Written in 1925, but only published posthumously in Phoenix *(1936).*

We have curious ideas of ourselves. We think of ourselves as a body with a spirit in it, or a body with a soul in it, or a body with a mind in it. *Mens sana in corpore sano.*[1] The years drink up the wine, and at last throw the bottle away, the body, of course, being the bottle.

It is a funny sort of superstition. Why should I look at my hand, as it so cleverly writes these words, and decide that it is a mere nothing compared to the mind that directs it? Is there really any huge difference between my hand and my brain? Or my mind? My hand is alive, it flickers with a life of its own. It meets all the strange universe in touch, and learns a vast number of things, and knows a vast number of things. My hand, as it writes these words, slips gaily along, jumps like a grasshopper to dot an *i*, feels the table rather cold, gets a little bored if I write too long, has its own rudiments of thought, and is just as much *me* as is my brain, my mind, or my soul. Why should I imagine that there is a *me* which is more *me* than my hand is? Since my hand is absolutely alive, me alive.

Whereas, of course, as far as I am concerned, my pen isn't alive at all. My pen *isn't me* alive. Me alive ends at my finger-tips.

Whatever is me alive is me. Every tiny bit of my hands is alive, every little freckle and hair and fold of skin. And whatever is me alive is me. Only my finger-nails, those ten little weapons between me and an inanimate universe, they cross the mysterious Rubicon between me alive and things like my pen, which are not alive, in my own sense.

So, seeing my hand is all alive, and me alive, wherein is it just a bottle, or a jug, or a tin can, or a vessel of clay, or any of the rest of that nonsense? True, if I cut it it will bleed, like a can of cherries. But then the skin that is cut, and the veins that bleed, and the bones that should never be seen, they are all just as alive as the blood that flows. So the tin can business, or vessel of clay, is just bunk.

And that's what you learn, when you're a novelist. And that's what you are very liable *not* to know, if you're a parson, or a philosopher, or a scientist, or a stupid person. If you're a parson, you talk about souls in heaven. If you're a novelist, you know that paradise is in the palm of your hand, and on the end of your nose, because both are alive; and alive, and man alive, which is more than you can say, for certain, of paradise. Paradise is after life, and I for one am not keen on anything that is *after* life. If you are a philosopher, you talk about infinity, and the pure spirit which knows all things. But if you pick up a novel, you realise immediately that infinity is just a handle to this self-same jug of a body of mine; while as for knowing, if I find my finger in the fire, I know that fire burns, with a knowledge so emphatic and vital, it leaves Nirvana merely a conjecture. Oh, yes, my body, me alive, *knows*, and knows intensely. And as for the sum of all knowledge, it can't be anything more than an accumulation of all the things I know in the body, and you, dear reader, know in the body.

These damned philosophers, they talk as if they suddenly went off in steam, and were then much more important than they are when they're in their shirts. It is nonsense. Every man, philosopher included, ends in his own finger-tips. That's the end of his man alive. As for the words and thoughts and sighs and aspirations that fly from him, they are so many tremulations in the ether, and not alive at all. But if the tremulations reach another man alive, he may receive them into his life, and his life may take on a new colour, like a chameleon creeping from a brown rock on to a green leaf. All very well and good. It still doesn't alter the fact that the so-called spirit, the message or teaching of the philosopher or the saint, isn't alive at all, but just a tremulation upon the ether, like a radio message. All this spirit stuff is just tremulations upon the ether. If you, as man alive, quiver from the tremulation of the ether into new life, that is because you are man alive, and you take sustenance and stimulation into your alive man in a myriad ways. But to say that the message, or the spirit which is communicated to you, is more important than your living body, is nonsense. You might as well say that the potato at dinner was more important.

Nothing is important but life. And for myself, I can absolutely see life nowhere but in the living. Life with a capital L is only man alive. Even a cabbage in the rain is cabbage alive. All things that are alive are amazing. And all things that are dead are subsidiary to the living. Better a live dog than a dead lion. But better a live lion than a live dog. *C'est la vie!*

It seems impossible to get a saint, or a philosopher, or a scientist, to stick to this simple truth. They are all, in a sense, renegades. The saint wishes to offer himself up as spiritual food for the multitude. Even Francis of Assisi turns himself into a sort of angel-cake, of which anyone may take a slice. But an angel-cake is rather less than man alive. And poor St. Francis might well apologise to his body, when he is dying: 'Oh, pardon me, my body, the wrong I did you through the years!' It was no wafer, for others to eat.

The philosopher, on the other hand, because he can think, decides that nothing but thoughts matter. It is as if a rabbit, because he can make little pills, should decide that nothing but little pills matter. As for the scientist, he has absolutely no use for me so long as I am man alive. To the scientist, I am dead. He puts under the microscope a bit of dead me, and calls it me. He takes me to pieces, and says first one piece, and then another piece, is me. My heart, my liver, my stomach have all been scientifically me, according to the scientist; and nowadays I am either a brain, or nerves, or glands, or something more up-to-date in the tissue line.

Now I absolutely flatly deny that I am a soul, or a body, or a mind, or an intelligence, or a brain, or a nervous system, or a bunch of glands, or any of the rest of these bits of me. The whole is greater than the part. And therefore, I, who am man alive, am greater than my soul, or spirit, or body, or mind, or consciousness, or anything else that is merely a part of me. I am a man and alive. I am man alive, and as long as I can, I intend to go on being man alive.

For this reason I am a novelist. And being a novelist, I consider myself superior to the saint, the scientist, the philosopher, and the poet, who are all great masters of different bits of man alive, but never get the whole hog.

The novel is the one bright book of life. Books are not life. They are only tremulations on the ether. But the novel as a tremulation can make the whole man alive tremble. Which is more than poetry, philosophy, science, or any other book-tremulation can do.

The novel is the book of life. In this sense, the Bible is a great confused novel. You may say, it is about God. But it is really about man alive. Adam, Eve, Sarai, Abraham, Isaac, Jacob, Samuel, David, Bath-Sheba, Ruth, Esther, Solomon, Job, Isaiah, Jesus, Mark, Judas, Paul, Peter: what is it but man alive, from start to finish? Man alive, not mere bits. Even the Lord is another man alive, in a burning bush, throwing the tablets of stone at Moses's head.

I do hope you begin to get my idea, why the novel is supremely important, as a tremulation on the ether. Plato makes the perfect ideal being tremble in me. But that's only a bit of me. Perfection is only a bit, in the strange make-up of man alive. The Sermon on the Mount makes the selfless spirit of me quiver. But that, too, is only a bit of me. The Ten Commandments set the old Adam shivering in me, warning me that I am a thief and a murderer, unless I watch it. But even the old Adam is only a bit of me.

I very much like all these bits of me to be set trembling with life and the wisdom of life. But I do ask that the whole of me shall tremble in its wholeness, some time or other.

And this, of course, must happen in me, living.

But as far as it can happen from a communication, it can only happen when a whole novel communicates itself to me. The Bible–but *all* the Bible–and Homer, and Shakespeare: these are the supreme old novels. These are all things to all men. Which means that in their wholeness they affect the whole man alive, which is the man himself, beyond any part of him. They set the whole tree trembling with a new access of life, they do not just stimulate growth in one direction.

I don't want to grow in any one direction any more. And, if I can help it, I don't want to stimulate anybody else into some particular direction. A particular direction ends in a *cul-de-sac*. We're in a *cul-de-sac* at present.

I don't believe in any dazzling revelation, or in any supreme Word. 'The grass withereth, the flower fadeth, but the Word of the Lord shall stand for ever.' That's the kind of stuff we've drugged ourselves with. As a matter of fact, the grass withereth, but comes up all the greener for that reason, after the rains. The flower fadeth, and therefore the bud opens. But the Word of the Lord, being man-uttered and a mere vibration on the ether, becomes staler and staler, more and more boring, till at last we turn a deaf ear and it ceases to exist, far more finally than any withered grass. It is grass that renews its youth like the eagle, not any Word.

We should ask for no absolutes, or absolute. Once and for all and for ever, let us have done with the ugly imperialism of any absolute. There is no absolute good, there is nothing absolutely right. All things flow and change, and even change is not absolute. The whole is a strange assembly of apparently incongruous parts, slipping past one another.

Me, man alive, I am a very curious assembly of incongruous parts. My yea! of today is oddly different from my yea! of yesterday. My tears of tomorrow will have nothing to do with my tears of a year ago. If the one I love remains unchanged and unchanging, I shall cease to love her. It is only because she changes and startles me into change and defies my inertia, and is herself staggered in her inertia by my changing, that I can continue to love her. If she stayed put, I might as well love the pepper-pot.

In all this change, I maintain a certain integrity. But woe betide me if I try to put my finger on it. If I say of myself, I am this, I am that!–then, if I stick to it, I turn into a stupid fixed thing like a lamp-post. I shall never know wherein lies my integrity, my individuality, my me. I *can* never know it. It is useless to talk about my ego. That only means that I have made up an *idea* of myself, and that I am trying to cut myself out to pattern. Which is no good. You can cut your cloth to fit your coat, but you can't clip bits off your living body, to trim it down to your idea. True, you can put yourself into ideal corsets. But even in ideal corsets, fashions change.

Let us learn from the novel. In the novel, the characters can do nothing but *live*. If they keep on being good, according to pattern, or bad, according to pattern, or even volatile, according to pattern, they cease to live, and the novel falls dead. A character in a novel has got to live, or it is nothing.

We, likewise, in life have got to live, or we are nothing.

What we mean by living is, of course, just as indescribable as what we mean by *being*. Men get ideas into their heads, of what they mean by Life, and they proceed to cut life out to pattern. Sometimes they go into the desert to seek God, sometimes they go into the desert to seek cash, sometimes it is wine, woman, and song, and again it is water, political reform, and votes. You never know what it will be next: from killing your neighbour with hideous bombs and gas that tears the lungs, to supporting a Foundlings' Home and preaching infinite Love, and being co-respondent in a divorce.

In all this wild welter, we need some sort of guide. It's no good inventing Thou Shalt Nots!

What then? Turn truly, honourably to the novel, and see wherein you are man alive, and wherein you are dead man in life. You may love a woman as man alive, and you may be making love to a woman as sheer dead man in life. You may eat your dinner as man alive, or as a mere masticating corpse. As man alive you may have a shot at your enemy. But as a ghastly simulacrum of life you may be firing bombs into men who are neither your enemies nor your friends, but just things you are dead to. Which is criminal, when the things happen to be alive.

To be alive, to be man alive, to be whole man alive: that is the point. And at its best, the novel, and the novel supremely, can help you. It can help you not to be dead man in life. So much of a man walks about dead and a carcass in the street and house, today: so much of women is merely dead. Like a pianoforte with half the notes mute.

But in the novel you can see, plainly, when the man goes dead, the woman goes inert. You can develop an instinct for life, if you will, instead of a theory of right and wrong, good and bad.

In life, there is right and wrong, good and bad, all the time. But what is right in one case is wrong in another. And in the novel you see one man becoming a corpse, because of his so-called goodness, another going dead because of his so-called wickedness. Right and wrong is an instinct: but an instinct of the whole consciousness in a man, bodily, mental, spiritual at once. And only in the novel are *all* things given full play, or at least, they may be given full play, when we realise that life itself, and not inert safety, is the reason for living. For out of the full play of all things emerges the only thing that is anything, the wholeness of a man, the wholeness of a woman, man alive, and live woman.

1   'A sound mind in a sound body'. Juvenal, (*c.* AD 60-130) *Satires,* X, 356.

I.A. Richards

Ivor Armstrong Richards (1893-1979), critic and theorist. He co-operated with C.K. Ogden in writing The Foundations of Aesthetics *(1922) and* The Meaning of Meaning *(1923), and also wrote* The Principles of Literary Criticism *(1924) and* Practical Criticism *(1929).*

22. 'The Poetry of T.S. Eliot', 1926

First published as 'Mr. Eliot's Poems' in New Statesman XXVI *(20 Feb. 1926), 589-5; then as appendix to the second edition of* The Principles of Literary Criticism *(1926).*

We too readily forget that, unless something is very wrong with our civilisation, we should be producing three equal poets at least for every poet of high rank in our great-great-grandfathers' day. Something must indeed be wrong; and since Mr. Eliot is one of the very few poets that current conditions have not overcome, the difficulties which he has faced, and the cognate difficulties which his readers encounter, repay study.

Mr. Eliot's poetry has occasioned an unusual amount of irritated or enthusiastic bewilderment. The bewilderment has several sources. The most formidable is the unobtrusiveness, in some cases the absence, of any coherent intellectual thread upon which the items of the poem are strung. A reader of 'Gerontion,' of 'Preludes,' or of 'The Waste Land,' may, if he will, after repeated readings, introduce such a thread. Another reader after much effort may fail to contrive one. But in either case energy will have been misapplied. For the items are united by the accord, contrast, and interaction of their emotional effects, not by an intellectual scheme that analysis must work out. The value lies in the unified response which this interaction creates in the right reader. The only intellectual activity required takes place in the realisation of the separate items. We can, of course, make a 'rationalisation' of the whole experience, as we can of any experience. If we do, we are adding something which does not belong to the poem.

Such a logical scheme is, at best, a scaffolding that vanishes when the poem is constructed. But we have so built into our nervous systems a demand for intellectual coherence, even in poetry, that we find a difficulty in doing without it.

This point may be misunderstood, for the charge most usually brought against Mr. Eliot's poetry is that it is overintellectualised. One reason for this is his use of allusion. A reader who in one short poem picks up allusions to *The Aspern Papers*,[1] *Othello*, 'A Toccata of Galuppi's,'[2] Marston,[3] *The Phoenix and the Turtle*,[4] *Antony and Cleopatra* (twice), 'The Extasie,'[5] *Macbeth*, *The Merchant of Venice*, and Ruskin, feels that his wits are being unusually well exercised. He may easily leap to the conclusion that the basis of the poem is in wit also. But this would be a mistake. These things come in, not that the reader may be ingenious or admire the writer's erudition (this last accusation has tempted several critics to disgrace themselves), but for the sake of the emotional aura which they bring and the attitudes they incite. Allusion in Mr. Eliot's hands is a technical device for compression. 'The Waste Land' is the equivalent in content to an epic. Without this device twelve books would have been needed. But these allusions and the notes in which some of them are elucidated have made many a petulant reader turn down his thumb at once. Such a reader has not begun to understand what it is all about.

This objection is connected with another, that of obscurity. To quote a recent pronouncement upon 'The Waste Land' from Mr. Middleton Murry:[6] 'The reader is compelled, in the mere effort to understand, to adopt an attitude of intellectual suspicion, which makes impossible the communication of feeling. The work offends against the most elementary canon of good writing: that the immediate effect should be unambiguous.' Consider first this 'canon.' What would happen, if we pressed it, to Shakespeare's greatest sonnets or to *Hamlet?* The truth is that very much of the best poetry is necessarily ambiguous in its immediate effect. Even the most careful and responsive reader must reread and do hard work before the poem forms itself clearly and unambiguously in his mind. An original poem, as much as a new branch of mathematics, compels the mind which receives it to grow, and this takes time. Anyone who upon reflection asserts the contrary for his own case must be either a demigod or dishonest; probably Mr. Murry was in haste. His remarks show that he has failed in his attempt to read the poem, and they reveal, in part, the reason for his failure – namely, his own overintellectual approach. To read it successfully he would have to discontinue his present self-mystifications.

The critical question in all cases is whether the poem is worth the trouble it entails. For 'The Waste Land' this is considerable. There is Miss Weston's *From Ritual to Romance*[7] to read, and its 'astral' trimmings to be discarded–they have nothing to do with Mr. Eliot's poem. There is Canto xxvi of the *Purgatorio*[8] to be studied–the relevance of the close of that canto to the whole of Mr. Eliot's work must be insisted upon. It illuminates his persistent concern with sex, the problem of our generation, as religion was the problem of the last. There is the central position of Tiresias in the poem to be puzzled out–the cryptic form of the note which Mr. Eliot writes on this point is just a little tiresome. It is a way of underlining the fact that the poem is concerned with many aspects of the one fact of sex, a hint that is perhaps neither indispensable nor entirely successful.

When all this has been done by the reader, when the materials with which the words are to clothe themselves have been collected, the poem still remains to be read. And it is easy to fail in this undertaking. An 'attitude of intellectual suspicion' must certainly be abandoned. But this is not difficult to those who still know how to give their feelings precedence to their thoughts, who can accept and unify an experience without trying to catch it in an intellectual net or to squeeze out a doctrine. One form of this attempt must be mentioned. Some, misled no doubt by its origin in a Mystery, have endeavoured to give the poem a symbolical reading. But its symbols are not mystical, but emotional. They stand, that is, not for ineffable objects, but for normal human experience. The poem, in fact, is radically naturalistic; only its compression makes it appear otherwise. And in this it probably comes nearer to the original Mystery which it perpetuates than transcendentalism does.

If it were desired to label in three words the most characteristic feature of Mr. Eliot's technique, this might be done by calling his poetry a 'music of ideas.' The ideas are of all kinds, abstract and concrete, general and particular, and, like the musician's phrases, they are arranged, not that they may tell us something, but that their effects in us may combine into a coherent whole of feeling and attitude and produce a peculiar liberation of the will. They are there to be responded to, not to be pondered or worked out. This is, of course, a method used intermittently in very much poetry, and only an accentuation and isolation of one of its normal resources. The peculiarity of Mr. Eliot's later, more puzzling, work is his deliberate and almost exclusive employment of it. In the earlier poems this logical freedom appears only occasionally. In 'The Love Song of J. Alfred Prufrock,' for example, there is a patch at the beginning and another at the end, but the rest of the poem is quite straightforward. In 'Gerontion,' the first long poem in this manner, the air of monologue, of a stream of associations, is a kind of disguise, and the last two lines,

Tenants of the house,
Thoughts of a dry brain in a dry season,

are almost an excuse. The close of 'A Cooking Egg' is perhaps the passage in which the technique shows itself most clearly. The reader who appreciates the emotional relevance of the title has the key to the later poems in his hand. I take Pipit to be the retired nurse of the hero of the poem, and *Views of the Oxford Colleges* to be the, still treasured, present which he sent her when he went up to the University. The middle section of the poem I read as a specimen of the rather withered pleasantry in which contemporary culture has culminated and beyond which it finds much difficulty in passing. The final section gives the contrast which is pressed home by the title. Even the most mature egg was new laid once. The only other title of equal significance that I can recall is Mrs. Wharton's *The Age of Innocence*,[9] which might well be studied in this connection. 'The Waste Land' and 'The Hollow Men' (the most beautiful of Mr. Eliot's poems, and in the last section a new development) are purely a 'music of ideas,' and the pretence of a continuous thread of associations is dropped.

How this technique lends itself to misunderstandings we have seen. But many readers who have failed in the end to escape bewilderment have begun by finding on almost every line that Mr. Eliot has written–if we except certain youthful poems on American topics–that personal stamp which is the hardest thing for the craftsman to imitate and perhaps the most certain sign that the experience, good or bad, rendered in the poem is authentic. Only those unfortunate persons who are incapable of reading poetry can resist Mr. Eliot's rhythms. The poem as a whole may elude us while every fragment, as a fragment, comes victoriously home. It is difficult to believe that this is Mr. Eliot's fault rather than his reader's, because a parallel case of a poet who so constantly achieves the hardest part of his task and yet fails in the easier is not to be found. It is much more likely that we have been trying to put the fragments together on a wrong principle.

Another doubt has been expressed. Mr. Eliot repeats himself in two ways. The nightingale, Cleopatra's barge, the rats, and the smoky candle-end, recur and recur. Is this a sign of a poverty of inspiration? A more plausible explanation is that this repetition is in part a consequence of the technique above described, and in part something which many writers who are not accused of poverty also show. Shelley, with his rivers, towers, and stars, Conrad, Hardy, Walt Whitman, and Dostoevski spring to mind. When a writer has found a theme or image which fixes a point of relative stability in the drift of experience, it is not to be expected that he will avoid it. Such themes are a means of orientation. And it is quite true that the central process in all Mr. Eliot's best poems is the same; the conjunction of feelings which, though superficially opposed–as squalor, for example, is opposed to grandeur–yet tend as they develop to change places and even to unite. If they do not develop far enough the intention of the poet is missed. Mr. Eliot is neither sighing after vanished glories nor holding contemporary experience up to scorn.

Both bitterness and desolation are superficial aspects of his poetry. There are those who think that he merely takes his readers into the Waste Land and leaves them there, that in his last poem he confesses his impotence to release the healing waters. The reply is that some readers find in his poetry not only a clearer, fuller realisation of their plight, the plight of a whole generation, than they find elsewhere, but also through the very energies set free in that realisation a return of the saving passion.

1   By Henry James (1888).
2   By Robert Browning, in *Men and Women* (1855).
3   John Marston (?1575-1634), dramatist whose works include *The Malcontent* (1604).
4   By Shakespeare (1601).
5   By John Donne.
6   J.M. Murry, 'Eliot and the "Classical" Revival' in *Adelphi* III, 9 (Feb. 1926), 585-95; the paragraph actually refers to both *The Waste Land* and Virginia Woolf's *Jacob's Room*.
7   Jessie Weston's *From Ritual to Romance* (1920) is referred to by Eliot in his Notes, as is the importance of Tiresias.
8   Canto XXVI of Dante's *Purgatorio* deals with the sexually promiscuous, the characters Guido Guinizelli and Arnaut Daniel, and Provençal poetic technique.
9   Edith Wharton (1862-1937) was an American novelist, who published *The Age of Innocence* in 1920.

C.H. Rickword

Cecil H. Rickword (?1890-1931) was the cousin of Edgell Rickword, and contributed to the latter's Calendar of Modern Letters. *Malcolm Bradbury in 'A Review in Retrospect' in the* London Magazine *for October 1961 (later used to introduce the 1966 reprint of* The Calendar*) calls it one of the 'three great literary reviews of the 1920s', together with Eliot's* The Criterion *and Murry's* The Adelphi, *and claims that 'It had much to do with the growth of the modern movement in criticism' (p.vii); see the Introduction to the present volume, p.26 above.*

23 'A Note on Fiction', 1926

Rickword reviewed Elizabeth Drew's The Modern Novel *in* The Calendar of Modern Letters, *III, 2 (July 1926), 166-8, attacking the tendency to regard 'character...as a portrait of an imagined human being', and arguing on the contrary that it is 'merely the term by which the reader alludes to the pseudo-objective image he composes of his responses to an author's verbal arrangements'. He drew attention to the tendency of 'the new "subjective" novelists' (of whom he referred explicitly to Joyce) 'to rely for their effect not on set-pieces of character-drawing, but directly on the poetic properties of words. The idea of a character's consciousness is created in the reader by the exploitation of the emotive powers of language used to evoke concrete imagery and sensation. The idea so created has an unusual reality...' (p.167).*

   He developed the argument further in The Calendar *III, 3 (October 1926), 226-33, as reprinted here.*

Having briefly considered the notions commonly attached in the criticism of fiction to the vague term character, it may be profitable to examine the almost antithetical set of ideas it is customary to include under the equally wide term 'narrative' or its synonyms. The word has one quite technical sense, when it is used of the method of a book. Then it signifies that a course of events is related directly by the author or his mouthpiece, and contrasts with 'dramatic' or 'scenic', which indicate that events are rendered more immediately by dialogue or other representational devices. In this sense, however, which is descriptive rather than critical, the word is quite unambiguous.

The case is different when it is applied to the whole book to denote the action, as distinguished from the characters. It has an apparently greater critical relevance than the latter term on account of the more genuine objectivity of the quality it designates. But this advantage is only apparent, for the actual story of a novel eludes the epitomist as completely as character; few great works are not ridiculous in synopsis. And for this reason–that the form of a novel only exists as a balance of response on the part of the reader. Hence schematic plot is a construction of the reader's that corresponds to an aspect of that response and stands in merely diagrammatic relation to the source. Only as precipitates from the memory are plot or character tangible; yet only in solution have either any emotive valency. The composition of this metaphorical fluid is a technical matter. The technique of the novel is just as symphonic as the technique of the drama and as dependent, up to a point, on the dynamic devices of articulation and control of narrative tempo. But, though dependent, it is dependent as legs are on muscles, for the *how* but not the *why* of movement; and, interesting as functional technique may be to the mechanical minded and to workers in the same medium on the look-out for tips, the organic is the province of criticism. More important, then, than what may be called the tricks of narrative is the status of plot and its relation to the other elements of a novel, particularly its relation to character, in solution.

Modern opinion, commonly assuming that the novelist expresses himself primarily through character, tends to regard story as more or less incidental; either it is scorned as part of the 'good old compromise...for the entertainment of the reader' or it is looked on as merely the expository structure–the Aintree, as it were, of character or, in less serious connexion, a modiste's parlour elegantly set for the mannequin parade.

Hence, though it is stipulated that plot be organic, it is required to be so in the sense that it may be said to arise out of, or be determined by, character. When a book is found satisfactory, this fundamental condition is said to be fulfilled, and 'value' is attributed to it or quarried out of character. Only when an imaginative failure is perceived is the plot scrutinized and then only for the, as it were, temporal location of the lapse, whose occasion is still sought elsewhere.

This position is vulnerable from several points. In the first place, in any sense in which the terms used have a meaning at all, it is plain that character, that is, that idea of a human being that is carried away from a play or a novel, is a product of the narrative. Whereas it is impossible to attend to the barest recital of an event, or series of events, without calling up for oneself an idea of the persons concerned, an equally bare description of character invokes no such animated notion. In fact, it is impossible to acquire from words any idea of a person unless that person is defined in time as well as in space. That is to say, action of some sort is indispensable. But, though this be admitted, it may still be maintained that value, nevertheless, resides in the character thus created.

This is, in fact, the usual contention. Professor S. Gaselee, in an Essay on the Greek Novel in the *Daphnis and Chloë* volume of the Loeb Classics,[1] remarks that 'fiction is one of the very few of the inventions of man that have improved in the course of the ages'. 'Brought up', he declares, 'on good novels, we are bored with their rude predecessors of antiquity... Of psychology there is barely a trace... any attempt indeed at character-drawing is faint and rough'.

I am not concerned to defend Longus[2] and his fellows against their detractor. Certainly, they and their English imitators such as Barnaby Riche[3] and Robert Greene[4] very soon become tiresome. No more speedily, however, than Maurice Hewlett, whose *Forest Lovers*[5] is instanced in the same essay as an example of the good novels that formed the Professor's taste. But the reasons given for the condemnation are interesting. In part, of course, they are the indignant outcry of a sophisticated palate at being fobbed off with thin and pastoral fare. More than that, though, they are also the sincere lament of an unsatisfied appetite. The Professor would like some sauce, but he really needs meat.

If we offered him Homer, even Homer in an English prose version, we should hear, instead of these wails of hunger, the happy noises of prolonged mastication. Now, it cannot be contended that the addition of a little psychology and character-drawing to a chain of events makes all the difference between aesthetic starvation and satisfaction, but some quality inherent in those events. And it is this quality that is common to all great works of literature, in no matter what genre. It is a unity among the events, a progressive rhythm that includes and reconciles each separate rhythm. As manifested in the novel, it resolves, when analyzed, chiefly into character and plot in a secondary, schematic sense–qualities that are purely fictitious. Neither is an active element in the whole work in the way that melody and harmony are elements in a piece of music. Perhaps it would be less ambiguous to designate this basic, poetic quality by some such term as rhythm or development; on the other hand, plot or story do indicate its nature–that it is primarily a sequence of events developing in accordance with an inner necessity.

And it is the recognition of this inner necessity that constitutes the recognition of value. To call this organizing principle 'character' is to attribute essential importance to what may be no more than a secondary manifestation and is often, even on the face of it, inaccurate. Obviously, the *Odyssey* has this unity; but it does not proceed from Ulysses. So, too, has *War and Peace*; yet Tolstoy makes it, perhaps, even too plain that events develop quite independently of the people they affect, as well as of those who are trying to affect them. And Hardy, in this at least, resembles him. Ultimately, this rhythmic coherence springs from the writer's conception of life and the adequacy thereto of his vehicle.

Actually, then, character is, to borrow biological jargon, an emergent quality of the novel. It emerges from the story, which is itself structurally a product of language, eloquence. An attempt, however, to cut out this intervening stage is marked by the assumption that the novelist's primary creation is of character. And this also indicates what is peculiar in the scope of modern fiction.

By the classic writer, elaborating a given pattern, the individual is seen included within the metaphysical hierarchy, symbolized as Fate, gods, and mortals. To the romantic, however, the individual appears containing within him that hierarchy, so that the writer is compelled to invent his own pattern. And the remoter his experience from the common, and the more personal his values, the more difficult will it be for his creation to make contact with an audience. This task, however, may be left to the character who, however highly specialized, is to be assumed to be a human being with the emotional, etc., equipment common to such. Whether a sceptical audience that, unmoved by assertion, demands sensible proof will be convinced is another matter.

Historically, character, as we now understand it, is an outcome of the Romantic Revival, a movement that has been discerned by some as one of escape from the mechanistic and indifferent universe of science into the fastness of the individual soul and of an attempt to locate there the limitations that constitute value. In Professor Whitehead's words: 'The independence ascribed to bodily substances carried them away from the realm of values altogether. They degenerated into a mechanism entirely valueless except as suggestive of external ingenuity'.[5] (There is no reason, however, to suppose, as this phrasing implies, and as is so often suggested, that developments in the aesthetic sphere proceed as effects from developments in other departments of thought. The imaginative faculty being supreme, poets themselves, not science nor philosophy, are to blame for any decay of sensibility).

Such an abstraction of values from the objective universe involves a corresponding restriction of the scope of significant action. In the epic, it is the completed action that animates the bare recital of events and, by unifying them, gives it structural vitality. Since the end is ordained by Fate operating through the wills and passions of gods and mortals, their deeds and speech are adequate to the poet's purpose. There is no need to go behind them to explain their meaning; that meaning is what happened and its inevitability. (The epic poet, like the historian, has also the advantage that, since the events he deals with actually occurred, his narrative cannot be doubted on the score of historic truth, but has only to satisfy as to its imaginative truth, or arrangement, whereas the feigning novelist raises questions of probability. But he, too, pretends to the authority of the past tense, and no one is likely so far to forget the rules of the game as to object unless there is a defect in his arrangement also).

Problems arise, however, when the overt subject of a narrative is, not the fore-doomed destruction of Troy, but the integration of a Richard Myrtle. The scene of action being removed from the external to the psychological world, a technique is required that will manifest the otherwise imperceptible events. Further, a principle is needed that will unify those events when manifested. This principle can be identified with the individual, the 'character', and located, by the romantics proper in the emotions, by Henry James in the intelligence, by the followers of Freud–gentle Ruths, gleaning psychology's alienist fields–in the sub-conscious.

Linked to these questions is that of authority–the angle from which the story shall be presented. Henry James was the first to realize consciously and to state that the interior drama must be shown to the inner eye if it is to be emotively efficient. But it is not vision alone that confers authority; Homer owes his to no sleight-of-hand with the 'seeing-eye', but to the internal consistency of that which he offers to it. Nevertheless, visualization is necessary, and it is the problem of objectifying and setting in disciplined motion the subjective narrative that has occupied nearly all English novelists of importance since Fielding, and Richardson before him.

It is curious that, though the Romantics destroyed the poetic forms of the previous tradition, yet the novel continued for a considerable period to be written on Fielding's plan. This was, perhaps, largely due to the fact that in England the novel has rarely been the medium of first-rate creative minds and to the not unrelated lack of self-consciousness in the matter of technique on the part of its practitioners. And Fielding's extraordinary effectiveness encouraged such inertia. But the effectiveness of his method proceeded from its entire adequacy to its content, which did not include the individual sensibility. Fielding's attitude was primarily social; he saw people as units in society and estimated their actions by the resultant effects on that organism. Secure of an audience that shared his views, he was able to use objective narrative with authority, though only types emerged from it. Further, being conservative of a tradition that accepted the whole of life as material for art, he was able to base his story very firmly on experience. But for all its permanence and solidity, his art was not heroic, as he himself admitted in calling *Tom Jones* a comic epic. Fielding's single-mindedness, that enabled him to retain so firm a grasp on the more immediate aspects of existence, was dependent on a spiritual crassness that allowed him to remain content with the stuffy metaphysics of his day. The difference between tragic and comic art lies partly in the different attitudes adopted towards the catastrophes ensuing on a collision between individual and collective values. Of course, the great comic artist, such as Congreve,[7] takes his stand above society; his standards are absolute and his own, not those of the herd.

Now, it is the weakness of an art such as Fielding's that it is almost wholly typical. It operates by the setting in opposition qualities abstracted from men, so that the response it arouses is only partial. It has the veracity of correct analysis and the further truth of coherent re-combination, but the appeal is limited mainly to admiration. If the romantic attention to the individual had meant an extension of the field of perception, the attempt to particularize and subtilize Fielding's structure might have succeeded. Unfortunately, it meant not an extension, but merely a shifting of that field. Consequently, though along with Fielding's method, some of his immediacy was retained, it became increasingly more necessary to expound the meaning of action. Thus the plots of the Victorians became cumbered with a vast amount of not strictly relevant matter, essential to them for their 'meaning', but quite un-resolvable. For the difficulty in exteriorizing the movements of the individual sensibility is twofold. Outward actions have to be invented that will re-create, and not merely illustrate, inward happenings, and these highly particularized actions have at the same time to be universalized. The necessity for having regard to these two aspects constitutes the real problem.

Dostoievsky solved it by the violent conjunction of extreme realism in manner to extreme ideality of attitude, but he did so only at the expense of a tremendous amount of will that might advantageously have been liberated for other purposes.

Henry James is often given credit for having been the first to assert that events within the mind might be just as important as those without. The claim is hardly just, but he certainly was the first to realize that the interior drama might be rendered immediately by language without the intervention of circumstantiating physical action at every stage, that the word was as capable of embodying mental as physical movements, and that its latter function was useful only because of its superior vividness.

But James', like Fielding's, was primarily a social art. Truly, the society James contemplated was composed of members far more differentiated and sensitive to other's individuality than any Fielding could conceive, and it was his own creation. It is one, however, in which the maximum development is assured for certain impulses only at the cost of the almost complete omission of others–roughly, the grosser appetites Fielding handled so vigorously.

Thus, though James' narrative is autonomous, it is so only within the boundaries of a limited experience; his action is complete and self-sufficing because it springs from a single source, but it is ultimately invalidated by a latent dualism that is not explicit only because the intractable factor is altogether suppressed. (This suppression is not complete until his last period, but its progress can be observed in his earlier books). Hence the much extolled purity of his plots is actually of less worth than the impurity of those of the 'great' Victorians, in which the presence of large masses of unassimilated matter is evidence of at least an attempt to be comprehensive.

But James' skill in the manipulation of incident, the intricate technique by which events were arranged in varying degrees of relief so that the climax stood out in the round with the maximum intensity and immediacy, was one elaborated to dispose the most attenuated substance in the most substantial manner possible and was dependent on the prose that, apparently aimless, yet with certainty isolated and held up to view the fact on which James wished to dwell. Without it none of James' other devices is sufficient to give more than mechanical form to a novel, as appears from his imitators.

It is notable that Joyce uses no such devices. Nothing in *Ulysses* is, to use Mr. Lubbock's distinction,[8] reported; everything is shown or dramatized. But Joyce contemplates not only the discrepancy between actuality and individual values, between things as they are and as they appear modified by the sensibility; his irony springs from a more profound opposition–that within the subject, the contrast between actual impulse and the appearance that, too, assumes in consciousness. From this profoundly critical standpoint, he is able to exteriorize and objectify vast psychological tracts that as a rule lurk shapelessly outside the action of a novel, perceptible only as unaccountable influences that distort and hinder its progress. And regarding with an equal eye the response both to external and internal stresses, attributing no more value to the one than to the other, he is able to compel both into the same perspective and so set in motion events that, occurring simultaneously on both planes, are in themselves adequate and self-sufficient. Thus the authority and directness of objective presentation is secured for the subjective narrative, Joyce's unit being the consciousness, not its social crystallization, the character. Dedalus and Bloom are but symbols of disintegration; the imminent, never clearly apprehended Ulysses is the hero of this Odyssey, whose significance lies wholly in the completed action and its organic relation to the events of which it is composed.

1   Stephen Gaselee (1882-1943) was a classical scholar; his 'Appendix on the Greek Novel' appears in the Loeb Classical Library edition of *Daphnis and Chloë* (1916; 1924); the quotation is from pp.413-14.
2   Longus was the reputed author of the Greek romance *Daphnis and Chloë*.
3   Barnaby Rich (?1540-1617) wrote a number of romances.
4   Robert Greene (?1560-92) wrote several romances, including *Philomela* (1592).
5   Maurice Hewlett's *The Forest Lovers* (1898) was set in the Middle Ages.
6   From *Science and the Modern World* (1925), p.280, by Alfred North Whitehead (1861-1947), mathematician and philosopher.
7   William Congreve (1670-1729), comic dramatist best known for *The Way of the World* (1700).
8   In Percy Lubbock's *The Craft of Fiction* (1921).

Further Reading

It is assumed that students will be reading the fiction and poetry of the writers represented in this volume. Relevant texts are indicated in the Chronology of Publications at the beginning of the book, and in the headnotes to each writer, which also give indications of further critical reading, as does the Introduction. The reception of the Modernists' works may be studied in the Routledge Critical Heritage series, which provides full selections of contemporary criticism. Relevant volumes are:

T.S. Eliot, ed. M. Grant, 2 vols. (1982)
James Joyce, 2 vols., ed. R.H. Deming (1970)
D.H. Lawrence, ed. R.P. Draper (1970)
Ezra Pound, ed. E. Homberger (1972)
Virginia Woolf, ed. R. Majumdar and A. McLaurin (1975)

In addition, the following more general works may be useful:

ANTHOLOGIES
D. Lodge, ed., *Twentieth-Century Criticism* (1972)
R. Ellmann and C. Fiedelson, *The Modern Tradition* (New York, 1965)

CONSIDERATIONS OF MODERNISM
M. Bradbury and J. McFarlane, *Modernism* (1976; 1983), with full bibliographies
P. Faulkner, *Modernism* (1977)
D. Lodge, *The Modes of Modern Writing* (1977)
S. Spender, *The Struggle of the Modern* (1963)

Index

Italicised page references indicate a major article.